CROSS STITCH
and
SAMPLER
book

CROSS STITCH and SAMPLER book

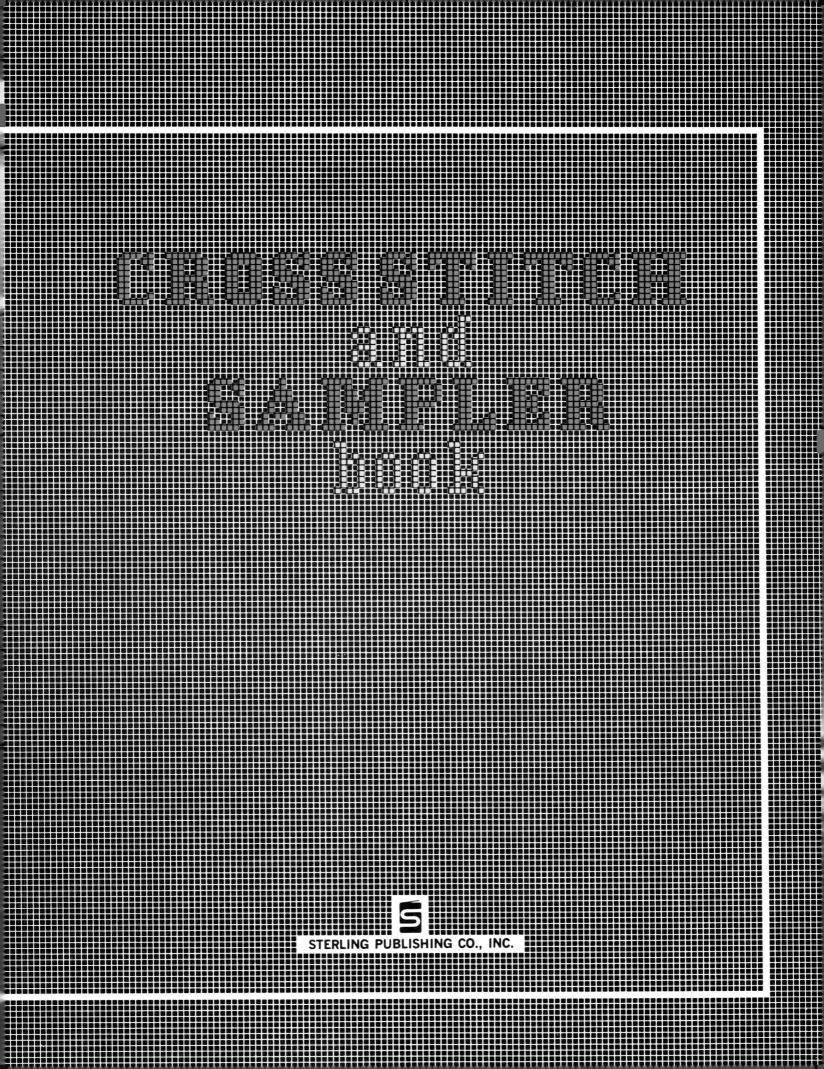

STERLING PUBLISHING CO., INC.

A QUILL BOOK

First published in 1985
Copyright © 1985 Quill Publishing Limited
ISBN 0-8069-5542-2

Published in the United States and Canada by
Sterling Publishing Co., Inc.
Two Park Avenue, New York, N.Y. 10016

This book was designed and produced by
Quill Publishing Limited
32 Kingly Court
London W1

Art director Nigel Osborne
Editorial director Christopher Fagg
Editor Sabina Goodchild
Project editor Judy Martin
Editorial assistants Dorothea Hall, Michelle Newton
Designers Mark Fuga, Fraser Newman, Annette Peppis
Illustrators David Eaton, Fraser Newman, Richard Phipps
Paste-up Carol McCleeve
Photography Michael Fear, John Heseltine

Filmset by QV Typesetting Limited, London
Origination by Hong Kong Graphic Arts Service Centre Limited, Hong Kong
Printed by Leefung Asco Printers Limited, Hong Kong

AUTHORS' ACKNOWLEDGMENTS
The authors would like to extend special thanks to the following:
Beverley Clark; John Gillow; Emma Kerr; Nicky Kerr; Hilary Mundle;
Sara Mundle; Brian Robinson; Chris Rushton; Eirian Short and Amy Speak.

Quill would also like to extend thanks to The American Museum, Bath;
The Danish House; Fitzwilliam Museum, Cambridge; Goldsmiths' College
Textile Collection; Victoria and Albert Museum, London.

CONTENTS

The art of cross stitch 7

Materials and techniques 21

Stitch directory 41

The projects 69

Samplers 105

Motifs 133

Alphabets and motifs — a directory of patterns 144

Glossary 154

Index 156

Acknowledgments 160

The Art of Cross Stitch

Embroidery is the art of enriching a background fabric with a wide variety of stitches in order to decorate it and create something beautiful. Over many centuries it has been an art practiced by both rich and poor, amateur and professional — to mark household linen and personal possessions; to embellish clothing and accessories; to decorate furnishings or add ornate detail to ceremonial robes and banners. Designs for embroidery can be infinitely wide ranging, according to the creativity of individual embroiderers, but it is a craft with a long tradition. The same motifs and stitches are used worldwide, yet there are also patterns and designs characteristic of particular regions or periods of history.

The richness of embroidery comes from the development of fine detail and even the most elaborate designs are constructed from relatively simple elements. Cross stitch is one of the oldest forms of embroidery; it has many variations and is a traditional feature of needlework in every culture. The present-day embroiderer can draw on an extraordinary range of work, as model or inspiration for new designs and interpretations. It is a pleasure to discover not only the inventiveness of the designers, but also the high technical standards of the many 'amateur' embroiderers whose work can be seen in both historical and contemporary examples.

The origins of decorative embroidery

The first simple stitches were used to join animal skins together, out of the necessity for clothing and coverings. The first threads were animal sinews or grasses, threaded through the skins with roughly-shaped bone and bronze needles. Examples of bone needles have been excavated that date from the Stone Age onward, and they are similar in shape to the needles used today. The first textiles were probably made from intertwined grasses and plant stems, until a way was found to twist short fibers and animal hairs into continuous strands by spinning. Originally the fibers were spun between the fingers; only later did the development of the wooden spindle and the clay whorl for weighting it make spinning into a mechanical process. Rudimentary spinning and weaving were practiced from about 10,000 BC and flourished in the neolithic settlements on the Nile Valley and the Indus Valley, and in Mesopotamia, Crete and China. From that period until the development of man-made fibers in the twentieth century, the raw materials for textiles came from four natural fibers: wool and silk from the animal world and cotton and flax from plants.

Each of the four early civilizations of the Old World, in Egypt, Southern Babylonia, India and China, seem to have preferred one particular fiber and developed its use. The Egyptians made flax into linen and the Sumerians in Babylonia developed the use of wool. Cotton was the typical fabric of India by 3000 BC and silk production was one of the great technical advances of early Chinese culture. Natural dyes also became important, although their colors at that time were very limited and overdyeing of two or more colors was employed to extend the range. The main plant dyes were woad in the West and indigo in the East, which gave a range of blues. Madder root produced a clear, fast red and weld yielded a yellow dye. Other reddish shades and the famous Roman Imperial purple were made from various insects and shellfish.

Embroidery probably began as a means of strengthening a fabric by darning in extra threads; it developed gradually into a decorative process. Fragments of cloth variously dating from between 5000 BC and 500 AD have been excavated from tombs and monuments in South and Central America, Egypt and China, showing crude examples of darning, half cross stitch and satin stitch. Many of these fragments are linen; the regular warp and weft of this fabric, one of the oldest of woven materials, provided the basis for development of counted thread stitches, beginning with simple half cross stitch.

The earliest known example of a complete cross stitch is thought to date from 500 AD or a little later, and was discovered in a Coptic cemetery in Upper Egypt. The embroidery is worked in upright crosses on a linen background. The scarcity of embroidery samples from ancient and early Christian civilizations does not

Below left This slipper is a piece of English workmanship. It has been embroidered in cross stitch and incorporates beads, which highlight the design to greater effect. Bags and purses were also worked in this fashion. *Bottom* This section, taken from a large, elongated band sampler, is another English piece. Completed in 1696 by Elizabeth Mackett, it is sewn in silk and linen thread on linen. *Below* This American sampler was dedicated to Lydia Noyes by her daughter, Martha, in 1806. Silk has been painted in watercolor, then partly embroidered in silk thread.

necessarily imply that decorative stitching was rarely used. Natural fabrics are perishable and could not have survived as have the metal and ceramic artefacts found in archaeological sites.

From the evidence available there is not enough accurate information to enable us to trace the precise origins of cross stitch. Some historians suggest that the development of cross stitch owes much to the craftsmanship of the Chinese, as this form of embroidery is known to have flourished during the T'ang Dynasty between 618 and 906 AD. From China, the skills and designs may have spread via India and Egypt to Greece and Rome, and from there throughout the countries of the eastern Mediterranean and the Middle East. Other schools of thought believe that the spread of cross stitch embroidery may have been in entirely the opposite direction, as it was notable that the first great migration of foreigners into China took place during the T'ang Dynasty. Persians, Arabs and travelers from Greece and India followed the silk routes to China and many settled there, influencing the designs used in Chinese arts and crafts, particularly those for textiles. Many Chinese textiles bear motifs that show great similarity to those found on Persian fabrics.

What is certain, however, is that from many of these countries the techniques and designs of cross stitch ultimately spread through Europe. The Crusaders probably brought home embroidered textiles from the Middle Eastern countries visited during the Crusades: the trade and spice routes carried not only articles for sale, they were traversed by emigrants who would practice their various craft skills wherever they settled. The dispersal of designs from their place of origin to so many different locations makes it difficult in most cases to identify any one pattern as having originated in a particular area, and the same motifs appear throughout the centuries in countries as far apart as South Russia and Spain, right up to the present day.

The development of cross stitch

Although cross stitch is now a common feature of needlework traditions throughout the world, there is little evidence that it was widely used during the period when decorative embroidery became an established practice among the rich and powerful classes of medieval Europe; for example, in the ceremonial vestments for Church and Royalty that were embellished with various forms of stitchcraft and design. One of the few surviving examples of cross stitch from that time is the badge of the Knights Templar, a military and religious order founded by the Crusaders, which forms part of the decoration of the Syon Cope (on show in the Victoria and Albert Museum, London). It was not until the sixteenth century that cross stitch and its variations were first used extensively, with the appearance of canvaswork hangings, tablecloths, carpets and furniture coverings. These were embroidered by the great ladies of the courts and castles, with the aid of their female staff.

The embroideries were stitched with locally produced woolen yarn or silk imported from the Middle East. A soft linen fabric, known as 'canvas', was most commonly used as the background. Cross stitch was worked in conjunction with tent stitch, satin stitch and other needlepoint stitches. Designs were copied from a number of sources — among them the woven tapestry hangings used as wall coverings. Contemporary portraits of that period incidentally record examples of fine stitching, in details of clothing and background hangings.

In the seventeenth century the pattern of life began to change. Women of this period, having a home-centered, comfortable lifestyle, worked more elaborate items of embroidery than before, less useful but more decorative. As travel and trade increased, and voyagers returned from the Far East and the Americas, many new design sources could be utilized. Strange flowers, birds and beasts found their way into traditional embroidery patterns. When translated into cross stitch, these designs often lost their original form and became decorative details rather than symbolic images.

The early forms of American embroidery, apart from the work of the indigenous Indian population, were developed from these traditions of European stitchery,

A typical use to which embroidery was put in the past is shown below. The panel (below) is a piece of English work completed around 1865. Cross stitch has been embroidered in wool and silk threads into linen, with the addition of glass and metal beads to supply a level of finery. Memorials commemorating personal bereavements were also popular among Americans in the late eighteenth and early nineteenth centuries. This panel (bottom) was originally painted, then embroidered. It is dedicated to the Moshier family and was completed in 1805.

Until the early part of the seventeenth century embroidery was mostly put to practical use. Costumes and furnishings were embellished with decorative sewing. This fragment (top) belongs to a table carpet or a long cushion cover. Colored wool, silk and linen threads have been worked in long armed cross stitch on linen. Religious cloths were also much embroidered. This section of a German vestment (above) dates from the fifteenth century.

Left These two modern panels are from Thailand. Straight-forward cross stitch has been worked on an even-weave fabric. The symmetrical, geometric design and lack of motifs are perhaps typical of contemporary pieces. *Below* With the use of beads and sequins this work is easily recognizable as Indian. It is actually the sleeve of a *chola*, the garment worn under a sari. The threads and fabric are silk. Both pieces show a well-regulated use of repeat patterns, but the treatments are different in terms of scale and color.

introduced as the settlement of America began in earnest in the seventeenth century. The types of stitchcraft commonly practiced at that time were canvaswork (now usually known as needlepoint), crewelwork, counted thread embroidery and quilting. Few seventeenth-century examples of American embroidery remain, but its existence is well documented. For example, an inventory of the estate of Governor Theophilus Eaton of New Haven, dated 1656, lists 'canvis and Turkey work' among other items of embroidery. Embroidered decoration was most frequently applied to household items, although samplers and embroidered pictures appear with increasing regularity in probate records after 1750.

The designs and materials available to colonial needlewomen depended to a large extent upon where they lived. Along the east coast, English and European patterns and high-quality materials were imported.

These included needlepoint canvases, yarn and fine silk fabrics. Further inland, materials were homespun: woven wool or cotton fabrics were used as ground materials and the stitching was worked in homespun woolen threads, colored with natural dyes. From the eighteenth century, linen cloth and linsey-woolsey, a wool and linen mixture, were produced from locally cultivated flax. The embroidery stitches used most frequently were tent, cross, flame and rococo.

As communications and transport improved, imported threads and fabrics became more readily available. At the same time, life became more leisurely and the emphasis swung away from the need to make mainly functional articles, toward a taste for more luxurious and ornamental items. Needlepoint was an increasingly popular pastime, especially when a craze for a type of embroidery known as Berlin woolwork swept through Europe and America during the 1830s.

Netherlands Early Dutch samplers reflected contemporary fashions and included tulip motifs within a few years of the flower bulbs being introduced to Western Europe from Constantinople. In Holland today, as in Scandinavia, many beautiful samplers are still embroidered on handspun linen.

England Popular interest in cross stitch embroidery is evident from the number of kits available for stitched samplers, pictures, pillows and table runners. Motifs include wild flowers and fruit, animals, country scenes, snow-flake designs and lettering.

Italy Assisi embroidery worked in traditional style is a thriving local industry today. It is a counterchange method in which only the background is worked in cross stitch, in a single color, behind motifs of fantastic birds and animals. The motifs were supposedly introduced to Assisi by St Francis on his return from the Holy Land in 1220 AD.

USA A currently popular subject for needlepoint samplers is the embroiderer's own house, adapted from a color photograph. Worked on fine canvas in appropriate colors and textured stitches, the samplers have a realistic effect.

Mexico Cross stitch is the favorite stitch of many Mexican peasants who still embroider traditional-style costumes. The designs, usually geometric bird and flower motifs, are worked in bright reds and blues on plain white cotton fabric.

USA (above) This is taken from an alphabet sampler completed by a 10-year-old American embroiderer, Nabby Ford, in 1799. The sampler has been worked in cross stitch and surrounded with a crewel work border of twining motifs.

Italy (upper right) Pillow covers were popular objects for embroidery. On this seventeenth-century example the background has been worked in red silk, leaving the pattern to show through as plain linen. Cross and long armed cross stitches have been used.

Eastern Europe In a Yugoslavian shawl (lower right) worked in cross stitch, the floral-style motifs have been cleverly used to fill out the right angle. An eighteenth-century Greek bed valance (far right) has repeating border motifs at the corners.

West Germany
Calligraphy —
including Roman,
Gothic, and script
lettering — is adapted
to the form of
beautifully designed
cross stitch alphabets
for modern samplers
and commemorative
embroideries.

**Greece and the
Greek Islands** are
famous for their
crossed stitch
embroideries,
traditionally worked in
home-produced,
bright-colored silks on
linen clothes and
many domestic items.
Large, complicated
designs are loosely
worked to give the
cross stitching a
characteristic raised
texture.

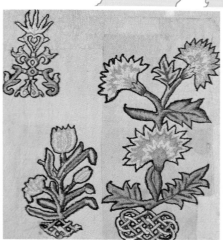

France *(above)* This
sixteenth-century
valance is a very
intricate piece of
embroidery. The
animal, plant and bird
motifs are cross and
tent stitches, in silk
and wool on linen.
England *(left)* These
plant motifs are
intended for applied
work. Colored silks
have been used to
sew cross and tent
stitches onto linen
canvas. The motifs
were stitched in the
sixteenth century, but
the couched brown
outlines probably date
from the eighteenth.

Turkey Several bright colors have been used in a border fragment dating from the nineteenth century *(left)* and definite motif designs, rather than the more dense repeating patterns often seen. It is cross stitched in wool on handwoven linen or cotton.

India Rich colors are often indicative of Indian work. This detail from the sleeve of a *chola (below)* is an unusual design, with the allover repeating motif.

Morocco The Sunni form of the Islamic religion prevents North African embroiderers from using human figures or animal motifs, although birds are used with other motifs such as the tree of life, flowers, stars and knots. In Azemmour embroidery, the background is filled with long legged cross stitch, around bird motifs left unworked or outlined in double running stitch.

Thailand *(left)* These pleated skirts were embroidered by members of the hill tribes of Thailand. The upper one is late nineteenth century, cross stitch with patchwork motifs; the other is modern, in cross stitch with ribbon appliqué.

USSR Cross stitch is the most widely used stitch in this vast area of different lands and peoples. Double running and Montenegrin stitches are also commonly used. Peasant designs show stylized figures, birds (peacock and double-headed eagle), horses, plants and geometric patterns repeated in deep horizontal bands.

China In rural areas, traditional blue and white cross stitch designs are still worked on white homespun cotton with indigo-dyed threads. Motifs and patterns have symbolic value — rabbits ward off evil, bats signify happiness, coins prosperity, and these are often embroidered on children's clothes, to protect the child.

Middle East The traditional woman's dress of the Palestinians, called a *djillayeh*, is richly embroidered with cross stitch patterns — usually in red silk on a dark ground. Small mistakes are purposely made in the stitching since it is considered unlucky to be too perfect.

Thailand Many northern hill tribes, such as the Yao and Meo, are prolific embroiderers who work beautiful geometric cross stitch designs on their national costumes, usually in bright colored threads on black or indigo cloth. Young girls practice working their designs on their cuffs.

Yugoslavia Peasant embroidery is often characterized by simple border patterns in just one or two colors. The section of a sleeve *(above)* is modern work but within a characteristic tradition. Dark and light blue threads have been worked in cross stitch to great effect.

India Much brightly colored cross stitch embroidery, worked in many parts of India on clothes and house-hold furnishings, is exported. Both Hindu and Moslem religions influence design, and colors are significant. Red and yellow are used for Hindu bridal wear to signify joy and happiness.

Middle East This piece of counted thread work *(right)*, in cross stitch throughout, has an extremely rich color scheme based on the contrasts of red against green and bright tones against muted shades.

15

Traditions of peasant embroidery

Cross stitch and its variations have been used all over the world for centuries. Motifs and stitches have for so long been exchanged between different cultures and geographical areas, through travel, trade and the wide availability of printed design books, that many of the geometric and pictorial elements are common property. Within basic categories, however, there are regional variations and interpretations that dictate the particular form of, for example, star, heart, flower and animal motifs. Since each basic shape is translated into the minute grid created by crossed stitches, there has been a gradual stylization. As most natural forms tend towards curves, the contours are modified by the angular emphasis of the stitching.

Although cross stitch has played a part in many rich and exclusive pieces of embroidery, one of its most important and widespread functions has traditionally been to decorate peasant garments and beautify household linens. Peasant embroidery has never sought to be more than a domesticated craft, passed down from mother to daughter. The stitches are very simple to work and the fabrics used — usually linen, varying in color from white to dark fawn and in texture from fine to coarse depending upon the locality — have been readily available to every household. The colors were often limited but the dyes very brilliant; two or three hues might be the maximum number, with the addition of brown or black for outlines. In China, peasant cross stitch is even today almost exclusively worked in dark blue thread on white fabric. Embroideries stitched in monochrome are perhaps the richest of all, as they show off the design to best advantage.

The apparently complex and closely worked border patterns which appear in peasant embroidery all over the world were achieved in the simplest possible way. Motifs used on their own are almost unknown; they are usually repeated to form border patterns stitched in rows, one above another. Sometimes as many as six or seven rows are put together to form an intricate design. These can vary from narrow to wide borders and it is rare to find more than two rows alike in a single piece of work. Greek stitchers have been particularly skilled in creating enormously complicated border patterns from fairly simple components. When sufficient depth of border was filled, the work was usually finished with a pattern that created a broken outer edge and, if further decoration was needed, single motifs were repeated above the border, widely spaced apart in rows or just dotted in at random.

Most cross stitch embroidery is worked on evenly woven fabric, but in some areas, in India, for example, where a regularly woven fabric was unusual, the designs in cross stitch were all spaced by eye rather than counted out. Most peasant stitchers were not troubled if the borders did not fit exactly into the required space; they adapted the patterns, added sections or missed out motifs, and these irregularities are an intriguing characteristic of peasant embroidery.

This free arrangement and the lack of design considerations as we know them give each piece of peasant embroidery its strong individuality.

The great value of studying embroideries from different parts of the world is that while some similarities can be identified, the differences are likely to be the most stimulating aspect for the practising embroiderer. One region may favor flamboyant, clashing colors while another specializes in the construction of elaborate combinations of motifs and borders. What is commonplace in one country is a diversion from tradition in another. This is an immediate source of new ideas for contemporary stitchers and can provide the confidence to risk unusual or unfamiliar techniques and design features. As the illustrated examples show, cross stitch embroidery is an extremely vital craft. Through embroidery's natural association with clothing, household goods and personal accessories, designs are continually refreshed by the marriage between traditions and contemporary preferences.

Above This is a typical example of a peasant-style design. White cotton has been edged with a series of rows of repeated pattern. The design is simple yet appealing, using geometric patterns and no definite motifs. This particular garment is a Yugoslavian dress from the nineteenth century, worked in herringbone and double running stitches.

Right The shape of this bonnet is of English design; however, the band of solid shapes topped with line patterns are indicative of embroidery of India. It is a nineteenth-century example of cross stitch, based on an English child's bonnet typical of the period, but actually executed by an Indian embroiderer.

Materials and Techniques

There are many different fabrics, threads and yarns that can be used for embroidery, but one of the beauties of the craft is the simplicity of the materials and techniques with which you can embark on quite ambitious projects. The first step is to acquire an understanding of basic equipment and methods — how to choose a fabric base and a suitable thread; the way to transfer a design from paper to fabric, enlarging or reducing it if necessary. It is important to be comfortable as you stitch and you may choose to work on a stretcher or embroidery frame. And when the work is finished, do justice to the time and meticulous effort you have invested by giving as much consideration to finishing and presenting the piece as you do to the design and execution.

Fabrics

Fabrics for embroidery fall into three distinct categories: common-weave fabrics, even-weave fabrics and canvas.

Common-weave fabrics

Only common-weave fabrics with a regular woven or printed pattern such as gingham, polka-dots or stripes will provide a useful grid for working crossed stitches neatly and evenly. The main exception is the herringbone family of stitches, which lend themselves to being worked freely on most common-weave fabrics including sheer ones. Basic cross stitch and some other canvas stitches can be worked on an unpatterned common-weave fabric, such as medium-weight cotton, provided a piece of canvas is basted over the fabric first, to provide a grid for regular stitching. When the embroidery is completed the canvas grid is removed.

The most important consideration in working embroidery on a common-weave fabric is to match the weight of the thread and needle to the fabric. The thread should not be heavy enough to distort the fabric weave or pull it out of shape, leaving puckers in the background. A firmly woven fabric should be chosen that allows the thread to pass easily in and out and is strong enough to bear the weight of solid areas of stitching without distortion. Knitted fabrics or loosely woven fabrics which stretch are not suitable for hand embroidery.

Even-weave fabrics

Even-weave fabrics, the second group, are also common-weave fabrics but there is an important difference. The warp and weft threads are identical in thickness and provide the same number of threads in a given area, enabling cross stitch to be worked accurately by the method of counting the threads. Single even-weave fabrics are made from single strands of intersecting threads; the thickness of the threads dictates the thread count. One of the most useful fabrics is an evenly woven linen, with a count of approximately 29 threads per inch (2.5 cm). Counted stitches can be worked over different numbers of threads depending on your preference for the size of the finished stitch. For example, basic cross stitch worked over three threads of a 29-thread fabric will produce just under 10 stitches per inch.

There is a large range of similar even-weave fabrics available, some finer and some coarser, and they are usually made from linen, cotton or wool, or blends of these with polyester or other synthetics. They are mainly produced in white, cream or pastel colors. Special types of even-weave fabrics suitable for counted thread techniques are Hardanger, Aida and Binca. Hardanger fabric has pairs of threads woven together while Aida and Binca have four threads woven together to form distinct blocks in the weave over which the stitches are formed. These fabrics come in different thread counts and are usually made of pure cotton, or cotton and synthetic blends. The color range is fairly extensive and includes pastels and bright colors such as yellow, red and green.

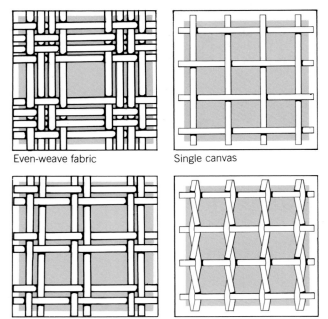

Even-weave fabric   Single canvas

Double canvas   Interlock single canvas

Canvas

The third fabric group consists of different types of canvas. Canvas is made of vertical and horizontal threads woven together to produce precisely spaced holes between the threads. The points at which the threads intersect are known as meshes and the fabric has a regular grid-like structure. Most canvas is made of stiffened cotton, but soft linen canvas and very fine silk gauze are also available. Rigid plastic canvas with a coarse mesh can be bought in rectangular sheets or cut into shapes. Cotton canvas is available in white, ecru or yellow. It is advisable to use white canvas when the embroidery threads are very pale as the stitching may not conceal the canvas completely; otherwise use ecru or yellow, as with darker-toned threads the canvas is less likely to show through the stitching. If you are using dark colors over a large area, the canvas can be painted to match to avoid any showthrough.

Choose the best canvas you can afford as the cheaper types often have knots or unevenly twisted threads in the weave which can distort the stitching. There are two main types of canvas: single canvas called mono, and double canvas known as Penelope canvas. Plain mono canvas is formed by the intersection of a single vertical and horizontal thread. Interlock mono canvas has a locked construction which makes it more stable than the plain canvas; each vertical thread is made up of two thin threads twisted around each other and round a single, thicker horizontal thread so each mesh is 'locked' into place. All crossed needlepoint stitches can be worked on mono canvas but some, such as the basic cross stitch and fishbone stitch, are more successful when worked on Penelope canvas.

Double canvas is similar to single canvas except that the mesh is formed by pairs of vertical and horizontal threads. Canvas comes in a large number of sizes, or gauges. The gauge of a canvas is the number of threads which can be stitched in an inch (2.5 cm); for example

24 gauge canvas has 24 threads to every inch. Fine silk gauze has a gauge of up to 72 per inch for delicate work, and the cotton canvases range right up to coarse rug canvas with a 3 or 5 gauge. If you work from a chart and use a larger gauge canvas than suggested, the finished piece will be larger; alternatively, a finer canvas will reduce the size of the piece. With needlepoint, it is extremely important to match the weight of threads with the gauge of the canvas to avoid crammed, bulky stitching or, if the threads are too thin, canvas covered unevenly by the stitching.

Needles

Needles for hand embroidery are of three types: crewel, chenille and tapestry. They have longer eyes than do needles used for plain sewing, to make threading a thick thread easier. All needles are numerically graded from fine to coarse, the higher numbers being the finer needles. Exact choice of needle is largely down to personal preference, but the eye of the needle should accommodate the thread easily and should be the right size to draw the thread through the fabric or canvas without pulling it out of shape. You will soon discover by 'feel' which size and type of needle suits the work you are doing.

Crewel needles — sizes 1 to 10 — are sharp, medium length needles with a large eye and are used for fine and medium-weight embroidery on common-weave fabrics.

Chenille needles — sizes 14 to 26 — are also pointed, but are longer, thicker and have larger eyes than crewel needles and are used with heavier threads and fabrics.

Tapestry needles — sizes 14 to 26 — are similar in size to chenille needles, but with a blunt end instead of a sharp point. They are used for needlepoint and embroidery on even-weave fabrics; the blunt end separates the threads of the fabric to pass through, whereas a sharp needle would split them.

Threads

Embroidery threads are made in a wide range of weights and colors. Some are twisted and must be used as one thread, while others are made up of several strands which can be separated and used singly or put together in different weight or color combinations. For cross stitch embroidery on common- or even-weave fabric, the following threads are suitable:

Stranded floss — a loosely twisted, slightly shiny six-strand thread which can be separated for fine work. A good all-purpose thread with an extensive range of colors.

Pearl cotton — a twisted 2-ply thread with a lustrous sheen, which cannot be divided. It comes in sizes 3, 5 and 8, 3 being the heaviest, and in a good range of colors.

Matte embroidery cotton — a tightly twisted 5-ply thread, fairly thick and with a matte finish. It is used as a single thread on heavier fabrics.

Coton à broder — a tightly twisted thread which is similar to pearl cotton, although softer, finer and with a less lustrous finish.

Stranded pure silk — a seven-stranded, shiny thread which can be divided. It comes in an extensive color range including many brilliant shades not available in stranded floss. It is also available as twisted thread, in a much narrower color range. Pure silk is difficult to work with and must be drycleaned.

For needlepoint, wool yarns are usually preferred as they are more hard wearing, with stranded floss, silk and pearl cotton introduced as highlights. For articles that do not require a hard-wearing finish, such as pictures, any of the previous threads can be used on by themselves. Crewel and Persian yarns are suitable for even-weave fabrics, providing the fabric is loose enough to allow the thread to pass through easily, without shredding or fraying.

The yarns most widely available are:

Crewel yarn — a fine 2-ply yarn for delicate needlepoint, in a wide range of subtle colors. Two, three or four strands can be used together on coarse canvas.

Persian yarn — a loosely twisted three-strand yarn which can be divided. Each strand is slightly thicker than crewel yarn and the colors are brighter.

Tapestry yarn — a tightly twisted 4-ply yarn used singly on coarse canvas.

Frames

All cross stitch embroidery, whether on fabric or canvas, should be kept taut during the stitching. The easiest way to do this is to pin or staple the fabric to a simple wooden stretcher a few inches longer than the finished size of the piece of work. G-clamps can be used to hold this type of frame securely on the edge of a table, leaving both hands free for working. Work on common-weave fabric can be stretched on a two-ringed circular hoop which can be moved easily from one area of fabric to another. More sophisticated frames, some with integral stands are also available. Good lighting, preferably from a gooseneck lamp, is important and you need a comfortable chair of the right height for you to work easily at a frame without overstretching.

Other equipment

Every embroiderer will accumulate a personal collection of particularly useful items of equipment and these may vary according to the type of work and the materials preferred. There are a number of general sewing aids which will invariably be useful — dressmaking scissors, a small, sharp pair of embroidery scissors with short blades, a thimble, a tape measure, ordinary sewing needles and threads for basting and a box of dressmaking pins. For design work and preparing the fabric you will need thumbtacks or a lightweight but strong staple gun; pencils, felt-tipped pens, markers and acrylic paints; a good supply of tracing and graph paper; a ruler and a T-square; and last but not least, a small mirror is a useful item, enabling you to work out reverse motifs and the corners of borders.

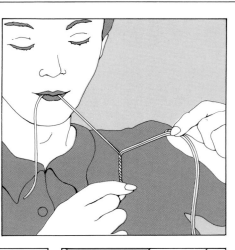

Separating stranded threads (*right*) Tease out one end of the thread and take two of the strands in your mouth, holding the other strands in one hand. With your free hand take hold of the other end of the thread. Gently pull the divided strands apart, while firmly sliding your other hand down the length of thread. It is important to keep this three-way contact to ensure that the threads do not tangle as they are being unraveled.

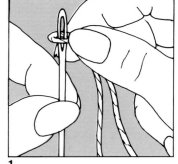

1

2

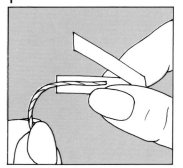

1

2

Threading the needle
Loop method (top)
1 Loop the end of the thread round the needle and pull tight.
2 Slip the loop off the needle and push it through the eye of the needle.

Paper strip method (above)
1 Cut a strip of paper, with a width just less than the length of the needle eye, and the length about 2 in (5 cm). Fold the strip in half and place the end of the thread inside the paper.
2 Feed the folded paper with the thread inside through the eye of the needle.

Preparing the fabric

Any type of fabric or canvas should be finished at the edges before the embroidery is begun, to prevent it fraying and to strengthen the edges for mounting the fabric in a frame. When working out the size of the fabric needed for a design, allow 3 in (7.5 cm) extra all round for unframed pieces and 5 in (12.5 cm) for framed ones. Cut the fabric to the correct size, using sharp scissors, following the grainlines or canvas threads carefully. To finish off the raw edges, turn them over and hemstitch them by hand or machine. On closely woven fabric the raw edges can be finished with a row of binding zigzag stitches. To finish and secure canvas, cotton binding should be folded over the edges and stitched down firmly.

Preparing threads

Working threads should be used in lengths of approximately 15 in (38 cm). Longer threads will tend to fray or lose their sheen because they are pulled through the fabric too often. A skein of thread can be cut into convenient lengths before you begin to stitch. Cut a piece of cardboard 15 in (38 cm) long, wrap the thread round and round the length of the cardboard, not too tightly, and cut through the thread at each end. Cut lengths can be loosely braided to prevent them tangling and each length removed as needed by gently pulling one end from the braid.

Threading the needle

There are three ways to simplify threading a needle, especially for coarser threads. The first method is to use a needlethreader — a flat piece of metal with a diamond-shaped loop of fine wire at one end. Pass the wire loop through the eye of the needle, place the thread through the loop and then draw the loop back through the needle, pulling the thread with it. If a needlethreader is not available, use either the loop or paper strip method illustrated.

Starting and finishing the thread

When you start stitching, do not use a knot as this may show through the finished piece or make a bump on the right side, especially if the work is to be framed. Anchor the thread by making one or two tiny back stitches in a space that will be covered as the stitching progresses. Alternatively, leave a tail of approximately 2 in (5 cm) of thread which can be darned in later. If you are continuing to work an area which is partly stitched, anchor a new thread by sliding the needle under the wrong side of a group of stitches, securing about an inch (2.5 cm) of the thread underneath them. To finish a thread, slide the needle in the same way under a group of stitches and cut off the loose end of thread.

Hoops (right) **1** To prevent damage to fine fabric, wrap a piece of bias tape around the inner ring. Make sure it is tightly wound, then secure the ends with masking tape.
2 Place the fabric over the inner ring with the design facing upward. Then place the outer ring over the top and adjust the screw so that it will fit lightly around the inner ring.
3 With your hands, gradually work your way around the ring, pressing it down over the fabric and inner ring, making sure the fabric is kept taut by pulling it outward with your fingers and thumbs.
4 You may find that the outer ring rides up as you are pulling on the fabric. In this case push the ring down over the inner circle so that it is securely fitted. When the fabric is evenly taut, tighten the screw to hold the outer ring firmly in place.

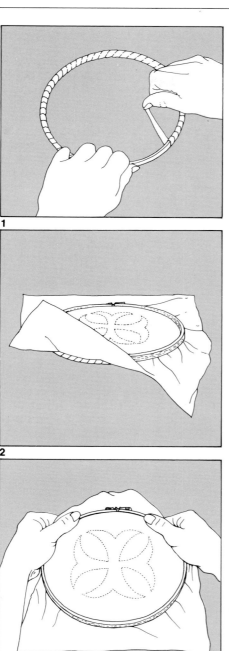

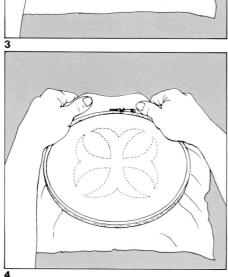

Using embroidery frames

There are several types of embroidery frame available, and the choice depends both on the size of the piece and your own preference. A hand-held hoop is adequate for a small piece of embroidery, but a large piece will require a rectangular frame with either a stand or clamps to keep it steady. A frame with a stand also gives the advantage that both your hands are left free for working.

Round frames
Round frames, or hoops, are used for small pieces of embroidery worked on common-weave fabrics. They come in various sizes, in two sections which are placed one inside the other with the fabric sandwiched in between. Some are tightened by a screw at the side. The smaller hoop, without the screw, should be bound with thin cotton binding as a precaution against the fabric working loose and sagging as the embroidery is stitched. The tape will also protect delicate fabrics. To mount the fabric, spread it over the smaller hoop and press the larger hoop down over it. Tighten the screw on the outer hoop slightly until it fits snugly round the small hoop, then ease the fabric with your fingers until it is evenly stretched and taut. Tighten the screw fully.

If the design is too large to fit completely inside the frame, the fabric can be moved along after one portion is completed. To protect the stitches already worked, spread a piece of tissue paper or muslin over the embroidery before it is remounted in the frame and cut away the paper or muslin carefully to expose the next area to be stitched. Release the fabric from the frame whenever you stop work for any long period; loosen the screw and remove the larger hoop.

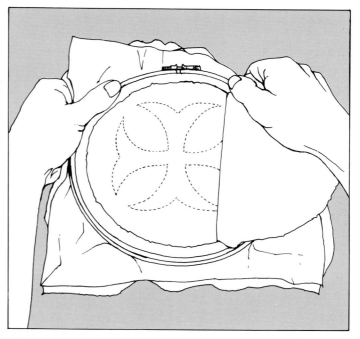

Protection of fabric or stitches (above) The rings may damage the fabric or stitching already worked. To avoid this, lay a piece of tissue paper over the fabric. Put the outer ring in place and secure it. Tear away the paper in the center.

Rectangular frames for all fabrics and canvas

The simplest rectangular frame is a wooden stretcher. You can make one from four wood battens joined at the corners, or you will find them available in many sizes from art shops. The size of frame you need is determined by the size of the fabric you are working on, as a stretcher is not adjustable. Leave a good margin on the fabric to make sure the entire area of the design is well clear of the inner edges of the stretcher. Mark the center of each side of the stretcher and the center of each edge of the fabric. Starting at the center of one side of the stretcher, line up the marks and pin or staple the fabric to this side, working from the center outward. Then attach the opposite side of the fabric to the stretcher, again working outward from the center, making sure the grain of the fabric is not distorted. Fasten the two remaining sides in the same way.

Scroll frames and rotating frames are more sophisticated than the simple stretcher and are bought from embroidery suppliers. They have the advantage of being adjustable and also of stretching the fabric very evenly. Each type of frame consists of top and bottom rollers with strips of webbing attached, and two side pieces secured with nuts, screws or pegs. After marking the center on both the rollers and the top and bottom of the fabric, stitch the fabric securely to the webbing, working from the center point outward each time. Use back stitch or herringbone stitch and a strong thread such as button thread. Slot the sides into the rollers, pull the fabric taut and secure the fixing device. If the fabric is too long, take up the slack by winding it around one of the rollers. Lace the sides of the fabric to the sides of the frame using a strong needle and fine string or linen carpet thread and leave a length of string at top and bottom. Tighten the lacing from the center outward, working each side alternately to give an equal pull on the fabric. Secure each end of the string by knotting it round the frame. It is important to get an even tension over the whole surface of the fabric, and several adjustments may be needed.

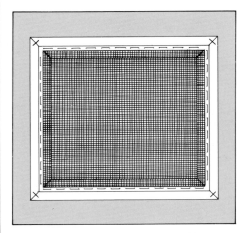

Canvas stretcher *(above)* This simple rectangular frame is made from four wood battens, joined up at the corners. The fabric is stretched and fastened lengthwise, and then across the frame.

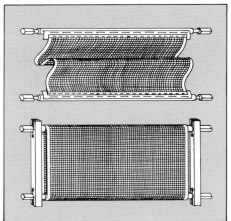

Rotating frame *(above)*
1 Sew the top and bottom of the canvas to the webbing.
2 Loosen the nuts on the side arms to open the slits and slot in all four ends of the side arms. Turn the rods to take up the slack canvas. Tighten the nuts on the side arms.

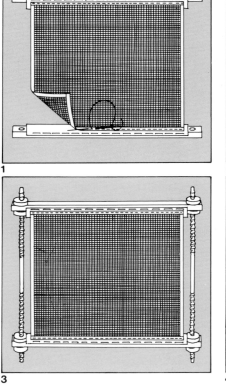

1

2

3

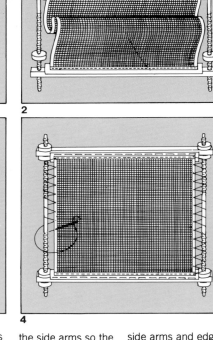

4

Scroll frame *(above)*
1 Bind the canvas to prevent the edges from raveling. Mark the centers of each rod and each edge of the canvas. Matching the centers, stitch the top of the canvas to the webbing on one rod, working from the center outward. Repeat for the bottom edge.
2 Fit two locking nuts to the center of each side arm. Fold or roll the canvas to just over half the length of the side arms. Slot the top of the side arms into the holes in the top rod; then slot into the bottom rod in the same way. Push the locking nuts toward the rods.
3 Draw the rods along the side arms so the canvas is fully extended. Push the centered nuts close to the rods and apply locking nuts to the ends of each side arm. Tighten the nuts on both sides of top and bottom rods to hold the canvas taut.
4 To stretch the canvas on each side, overcast between the side arms and edges of the canvas using long, slanting stitches. Before finishing the thread, pull on each stitch from the beginning of the sewing to tighten it and make sure the canvas is evenly stretched. Secure the thread at each corner of the frame.

Transferring designs

Before starting work on your piece of embroidery, you will need to decide how to transfer the design to the fabric. There are several methods of doing this, depending on the type of fabric you have chosen as a background. On common-weave fabrics, guidelines for the areas of stitching should be accurately drawn. If you are using cross stitch on an even-weave fabric or canvas, the usual method is to work from a color chart by counting the threads to determine the placing of the stitches.

Transferring a design onto a common-weave fabric

Using carbon paper This method will work well on smooth fabrics and is simple and quick. Place a sheet of dressmaker's carbon paper between the fabric and an outline tracing of your design, making sure the design is centered. Pin them to a flat surface and draw round the outlines with a hard pencil or use a tracing wheel for simple shapes. Use blue or red carbon paper for light fabrics and yellow carbon paper for dark fabrics.

Basting through paper This is the best method to use on an uneven fabric or a pile fabric such as velvet or toweling. Trace the design outlines carefully on tissue paper or some wax paper, center the tracing on the fabric and pin it in place. Baste round the traced lines with small stitches, using a fine thread that contrasts with the fabric. When the basting is completed, tear the paper away gently, leaving the outlines basted through the fabric. If the embroidery does not completely hide the basting when the piece is finished, remove the basting thread carefully using a pair of tweezers.

Using a light source This method works only with fine, smooth fabrics such as cotton or silk. Rest a sheet of glass or plexiglass between two dining chairs and place a strong light underneath the glass, pointing upward. A lamp with the shade removed, a gooseneck or similar adjustable lamp are best. Trace your design outlines onto tracing paper or wax paper and then fix this to the top of the glass with masking tape. Center the fabric over the tracing, securing it with more tape. The light will reflect the design on the fabric and you can carefully trace it with a sharp pencil.

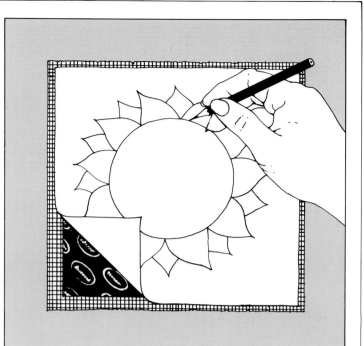

Using carbon paper *(above)* Having traced your design on tracing paper, lay a sheet of dressmaker's carbon over the fabric. Place the tracing paper on top of the carbon, making sure the design in centered on the fabric. Using a pencil, draw over the design. Make sure that you press firmly so that the design transfers to the fabric.

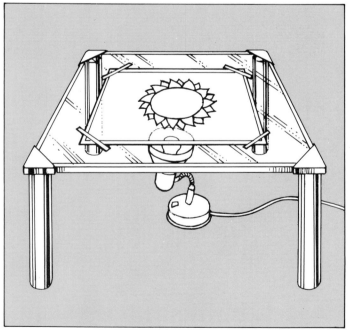

Basting through paper *(right)* Trace your design on tissue paper, then lay this paper over the fabric. Baste around the outline of the design, using small stitches to retain the detail. Tear away the tissue paper, leaving the stitched outline on the fabric. The basting may be left on the fabric underneath the finished stitching, or can be plucked out with a pair of tweezers.

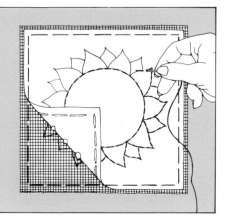

Using a light source *(above)* Having set up a glass-topped surface, place the lamp — or other similar light source — underneath, directing the light upward through the glass. Place the sheet of tracing paper, with the design traced on it, over the glass surface and fix it with masking tape. Take your piece of fabric and center it over the design on the tracing paper. The light shining up from below will enable you to see the design through the fabric, providing you are working on material that is relatively fine. Keep the fabric and tracing securely positioned while you trace the design. Use a soft, sharp pencil, to avoid damaging the fabric.

Transferring a design onto canvas

These methods are preferable to using a chart when you intend to work an assortment of stitches of different sizes on the canvas.

Outlines Lay the canvas over the design and fix it in position with pins or tape. The design will be visible through the grid of the canvas. Paint the outlines on the canvas using a fine brush and waterproof black ink. A waterproof ink must be used as the canvas will get wet when it is blocked before mounting.

Colored areas This method is similar to the previous one, but areas of color are painted on the canvas rather than just outlines. Use acrylic paints or waterproof inks

Transferring a design onto canvas
Outlines (below)
1 First establish the center of the design by drawing a vertical and a horizontal line across it. Mark the intersection at the center of the canvas.
2 Place the canvas over the design, matching up the center points, and pin the two together. Then, draw the outlines of the design

as they show through.
Colored areas
(bottom)
1 Draw a horizontal and vertical line over your design to find the center, doing the same with the canvas.
2 Place the canvas over the design, matching up the centers, and pin the two together. Paint each color in the design on the appropriate area of canvas.

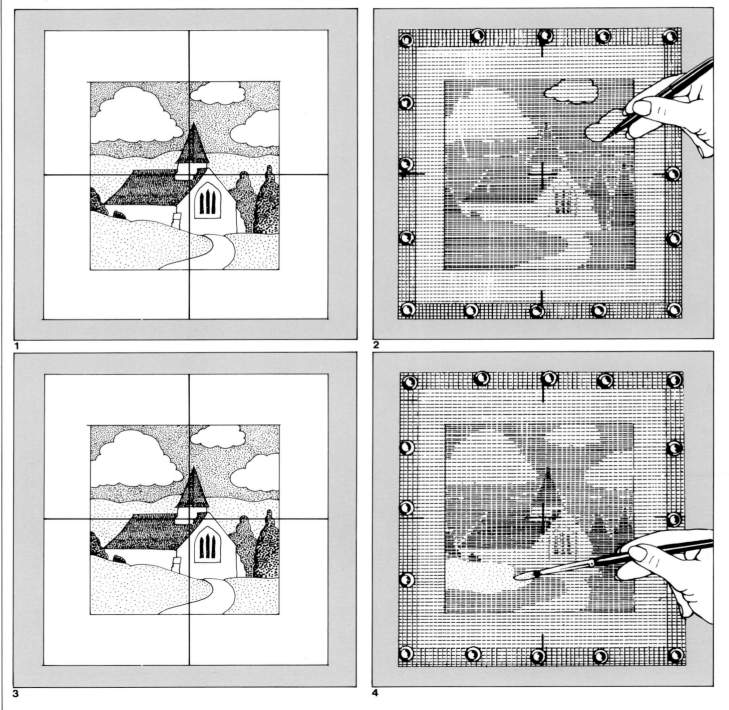

1

2

3

4

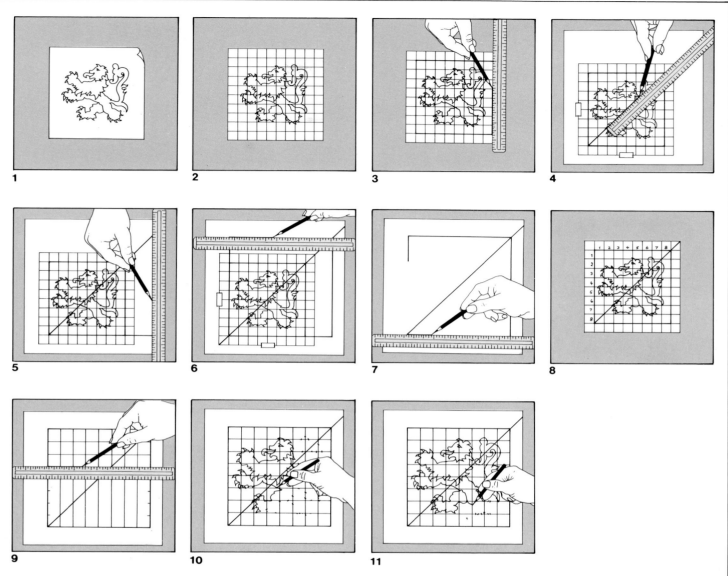

to paint the shapes, matching the design colors as accurately as possible.

With both these methods, you may find that the stitch you have chosen for a particular area cannot be worked right to the edge, as there is too little space left to fit in another complete stitch. The shape can be altered slightly to compensate for this, or the small gaps can be filled in with tent stitch in the same yarn.

Enlarging and reducing designs

When working from a charted design, the finished piece can be made larger or smaller by calculating how many stitches per inch (2.5 cm) you require for a particular size, and then choosing your even-weave fabric or canvas accordingly. However, you may need to enlarge or reduce the design before making a chart or before transferring it by the methods previously mentioned. Do this by squaring it up or down following the grid technique shown in the diagrams.

Enlarging a design
1 Trace or draw your design on to the center of a piece of paper.
2 Draw a small grid pattern over the design, with lines about ¼ in (1 cm) apart.
3 Using a ruler, mark the outer proportions of the shape on the grid.
4 Place the grid on a larger piece of paper and tape down the lower lefthand corner. Draw in a diagonal line from corner to corner of the design box, extending beyond the top righthand corner of the grid.
5 Extend the bottom line of the design box to the desired width of the enlargement. Draw a line at a right angle from this base line to meet the diagonal.
6 Draw in the top line to meet the lefthand side of the grid.
7 Remove the grid and complete the lines in areas covered by the original design.
8 Taking the original grid, number the squares across the width and down the sides.
9 Divide the larger box into the same number of squares as the small grid.
10 You can now reproduce the design by copying the lines from each square of the small design to the corresponding squares on the larger grid.
11 An accurate method of drawing the image is to mark where each line intersects a grid line and then join the marks.

Reducing a design
(right)

1 Trace your design on the center of a piece of paper.

2 Draw a large grid over the design, with lines approximately 1 in (2.5 cm) apart.

3 With a ruler, mark the chosen proportions for the outer edges of your design.

4 Draw in a diagonal line across the grid from corner to corner.

5 Tape a piece of paper, smaller than the full design, on top of the grid, securing it at the bottom lefthand corner. Extend the diagonal line showing at the top right of the grid down over the taped piece of paper.

6 Extend the bottom line of your original design perimeter to meet the diagonal in the bottom left corner. Draw a vertical line from this corner at a right angle to meet the line on the lefthand side of the grid.

7 Measure the desired width of the new design from the lefthand corner along the bottom line. From this point, draw a line up at a right angle to meet the diagonal. Then, draw a line at a right angle to this vertical line, to meet the lefthand side of the design, completing the box.

8 On the original grid, number the squares across the top and down the sides.

9 Divide the small box into the same number of squares, making a small grid proportionate to the large one.

10 and **11** To reproduce the design, copy the lines in the boxes on the original grid onto the corresponding squares of the smaller grid. It is easier to reproduce the design accurately by marking the points on each square where the design crosses the grid lines and then joining these points.

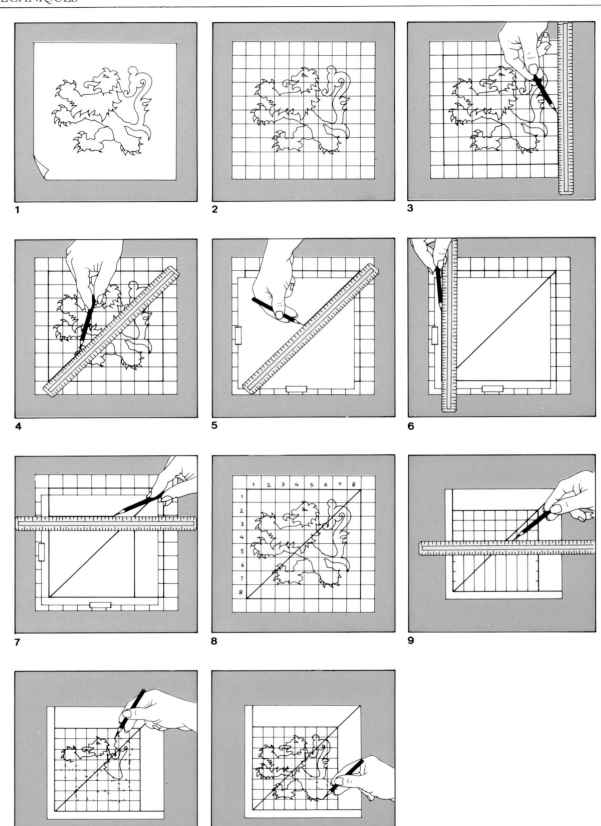

Charting a design

When you use cross stitch on even-weave fabric and canvas, the best way to follow the design is to make a chart and use it as reference for working directly on the fabric. You interpret the chart by counting the threads in the fabric. This method also has the advantage of leaving the fabric or canvas unmarked, so changes to the design can be made while the work is in progress.

Making the chart

The first step in making a chart of your design is to square it up onto graph paper. The easiest way to do this is to work on ready-printed, graphed tracing paper, or you can rule a grid on plain tracing paper. Lay the tracing paper over the design and trace the outlines with a fine black felt pen, adjusting the shapes to fit the printed squares. This will give you a squared outline design which you then copy square for square on graph paper. Color in each area using felt pens or colored inks. Do not use opaque paint for this process as it will obliterate the lines on the graph paper. Each colored square represents one cross stitch to be worked on the fabric. If you are using ready graphed motifs or borders to make your design, draw these directly on the graph paper to work out their placing on the fabric. Border corners should be worked out by using a mirror as shown in the diagram on page 137.

Calculating the dimensions

The finished size of the piece will depend on whether you work the stitches over one thread or a group of threads, and the gauge of canvas or even-weave fabric you have chosen. Experiment with stitch size and types of thread on a spare piece of background fabric to get the effect you like. You can then work out the finished size of the stitching. Suppose the design on the graph paper chart is 40 squares wide and 60 squares deep; if you plan to use even-weave fabric with 10 threads to the inch (2.5 cm) and work each cross stitch over two threads, you will fit five complete stitches into each inch of the fabric. The finished design will measure 8 in (20 cm) by 12 in (30 cm). Then decide whether you will mount the piece over masonite to display it, or frame it behind glass. For mounting and framing purposes, an extra 5 in (12.5 cm) all round is needed, so your piece of fabric or canvas should measure 18 in (45 cm) by 22 in (55 cm). If you intend to make the piece up into a pillow or tablecloth or it is a piece of fashion embroidery for use on a garment, a 3 in (7.5 cm) margin all round is sufficient.

Using a chart

Prepare the fabric and mount it in a frame. The first step is to mark the center of the fabric. From the half-way point along the top of the fabric, baste down to the bottom with a contrasting thread being careful not to cross any vertical threads. Mark the center horizontal by basting in the same way from side to side. Do exactly the same if you are using canvas. Draw corresponding lines across the chart to find the center. Begin stitching at the center of the fabric, working outward in each direction, following the chart square by square.

Blocking

Blocking is the name given to the process of stretching and smoothing out the distortions on a finished piece of embroidery. If the embroidery is on a common-weave or even-weave fabric and has been worked in a frame, blocking is not usually necessary. A very light pressing with an iron will be sufficient to straighten any fabric distortion. Before pressing, pad the ironing board with a thick, folded towel, lay the embroidery face down and cover it with a slightly damp piece of thin cloth. Press lightly, letting the iron just touch the pressing cloth. Do not press a piece that has heavily textured stitches worked on it, as they will be flattened. Block this face upward as with needlepoint, which must always be blocked even when worked in a frame.

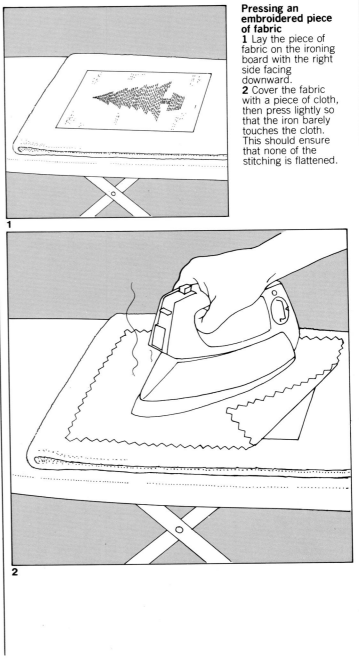

Pressing an embroidered piece of fabric
1 Lay the piece of fabric on the ironing board with the right side facing downward.
2 Cover the fabric with a piece of cloth, then press lightly so that the iron barely touches the cloth. This should ensure that none of the stitching is flattened.

Mounting directly onto masonite (*right*)
1 Place the embroidered piece on the board, face upward. Fold back two opposite, unworked edges of canvas, and put pins through the canvas into the outside edge of the board.
2 Turn the board over and, starting from the top lefthand corner, sew the two overlapping edges of canvas together with large interlacing stitches. With each stitch, go back to the starting point and pull the threads to tighten up the stitches along the way.
3 When you have reached the end, remove the pins. Knot the thread at the starting point and move along the stitching, tightening it up as you go. The fabric should then be firmly stretched.
4 Turn over the other two unworked edges of the canvas and sew these together in the same way. Make simple box corners. Remember to go back and tighten the stitches at each stage, making sure the canvas is evenly stretched.

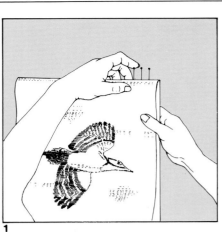

1

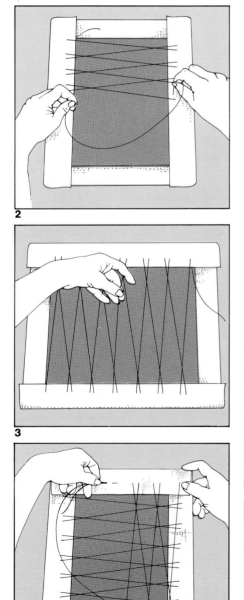

2

3

4

Mounting on board

This can be done in two ways. The embroidery can be stitched onto a fabric-covered piece of masonite, or it can be stretched directly over the board and laced at the back with fine string or linen carpet thread. The first method takes longer but is good for mounting work on fine, delicate fabrics or shaped pieces.

Framing

Once the piece of work is mounted, framing behind glass will protect it from the dirt and dust in the atmosphere. You can make your own frame, buy one ready-made or take your mounted piece to be framed professionally.

It is important that the glass does not touch the embroidered surface or the stitches will be flattened. To avoid this, small strips of wood, mitered at the edges, should be placed in the corners of the frame between the glass and embroidery to keep them apart. These strips of wood should be small enough not to show under the frame. An alternate method of separating glass and embroidery is to use a colored window mount made of acid-free cardboard. After framing, make sure a backing sheet (usually made of brown paper) is firmly stuck over the back of the frame to exclude all dirt and dust.

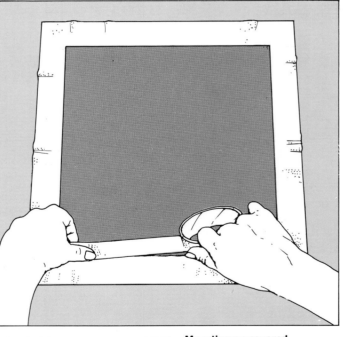

Mounting on covered masonite Cut out a piece of lightweight linen, allowing a margin of 3 in (7.5 cm) all round the size of the board. Stretch it over the board, fold back the edges and glue them down (*above*). Position the work face up on the covered surface (*left*). Stretch it evenly, pin it and then sew it securely to the fabric.

Framing (right)
1 Insert small strips of wood in the corners of the frame before dropping the mounted work into the frame. The strips of wood must be small enough to be hidden in the frame, but substantial enough to separate the stitching from the glass and thus prevent flattening.
2 To hold the work in the frame, hammer a fine nail into the center of each side of the frame, making sure the nails are angled over the mount.
3 Turn the frame over to check that the embroidered design is positioned, then turn back and insert several more nails at regular intervals around the frame.
4 Seal the edge between frame and mount with cellophane tape to exclude dust. Finish off with a protective sheet of brown paper glued or taped over the back of the frame.

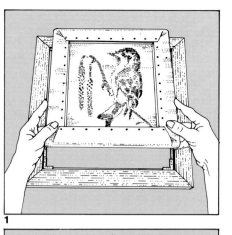

1

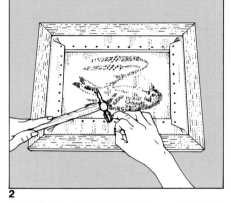

2

3

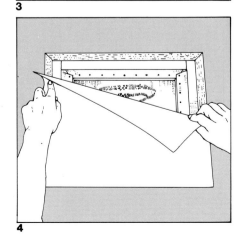

4

Displaying

It is important when deciding where to hang your framed or unframed piece of embroidery, to choose a position that eliminates the risk of damage during long periods. Always avoid hanging an embroidery where it can be faded by direct sunlight or bright lights. If you hang it over a fireplace or radiator, the constantly changing temperature and humidity will weaken the fibers of the fabric and damage the piece. A large embroidery can make a stunning centerpiece hung alone on a plain wall, or a collection of smaller pieces can be grouped together.

Designing with color

There are no set rules governing the choice of effective color combinations — all colors tend to combine and interact in different ways. Colors change according to their context; red on a black background appears very different from the same red on a white ground, and the effect would again be subtly varied if a strong contrast such as blue, green or yellow was introduced close to the red. In embroidery, the background color must be taken into account when you select colors for the motifs and patterns. Often this is the tone of the fabric — white, cream or grey, for example — but if you intend to stitch the background with a relatively strong color, such as blue, it will play a more complex role in defining the color relationships as a whole.

The background color need not be a single tone throughout. You can graduate the tones from light to dark, and this will again affect the values of colors used in the motifs. It is advisable to work out the color combinations on paper, as the result will depend upon the amount and placing of each color in the stitched design, and it is difficult to visualize this just by looking at a selection of threads.

You can find ideas for color schemes from a variety of sources — fabric and wallpaper designs, advertisements and fashion features, photographs and paintings, and the projects and samples shown in this book. There are some simple guidelines that suggest ways of organizing colors. Primary colors — red, blue and yellow — have opposites, referred to as complementaries, in the secondary colors — green, orange and purple — each formed by mixing two primaries. In their purest state, combinations of these colors are very vivid. More complex and delicate hues exist in further mixtures — red-purple, blue-green and so on — and in the range of tones derived from a single hue — for example, from dark red through scarlet to light pink. Tonal color schemes can be very effective as they give a natural continuity throughout the design.

Unusual effects can be created with discordant, or clashing, colors. One useful device is reversal of the expected tones; instead of using a light yellow against a rich, deep purple, try a heavy, dark yellow against pale lilac. Experiment with discordant mixtures of bold colors, such as orange with turquoise or vibrant pink.

Color can also be used to suggest space in a design. Bright colors in the foreground and neutral tones in the

The value of selecting a bold range of colors is demonstrated in this Indian cap *(below)*. The design is particularly successful because the same range of vivid hues is used in each section of the squared shape, but not distributed in the same way within the pattern. This arrangement creates continuity within the design, but due to the variations, the effect is never dull or predictable. The bright hues play against each other and are offset by dark tones of blue, green and purple, as well as black, which add richness to the tonal contrasts. The use of bright primary and secondary colors is typical of certain styles of peasant embroidery — as here, the heavy pinks, purples and blues are often a feature of Indian work — but more flamboyant color schemes are common in modern work from many countries. Dyes for threads and fabrics are far more reliable and wide-ranging than in past centuries, and therefore give greater scope to contemporary work.

background are a reliable choice, but you can create a more complex interaction by mixing 'warm' and 'cool' colors — red, pink, orange and purple against blue, green and grey. Warm colors seem to come forward, suggesting foreground space, while cool tones tend to recede.

Embroidery threads are available in an extensive range of pure hues, light to dark tones and neutral colors, including shaded threads that are specially dyed to provide graduated tones of a single color. As well as working out color schemes on paper, stitch small samples with simple blocks of color to see the effects of the actual threads, which may be subtly different from a design colored with paint or felt-tipped pens.

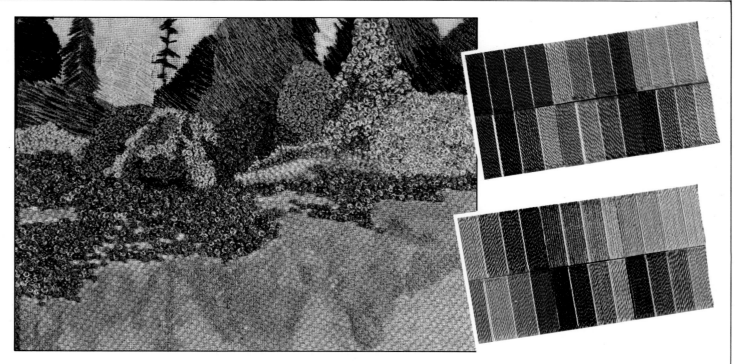

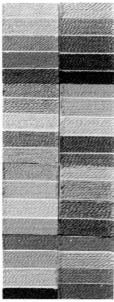

Color charts using actual examples of stranded floss show various ways of organizing tonal and color relationships. Heavy, warm colors *(top)* create clashing, discordant mixtures while muted, cool tones *(above)* have a neutralizing effect. Monochromatic color schemes are effective, in close tones of each color *(left)*, and seen all together provide some interesting contrasts.

Two very different landscape pictures show how texture also affects the color relationships in a design. Tapestry yarn and stranded floss are combined in warm sunset colors, demonstrating strong complementaries *(left)* against a solid area of black. Mixed strands of greens and browns give a painted effect *(above left)* and the illusionistic qualities are enhanced by the use of net fabric shadowing an area of dyed canvas.

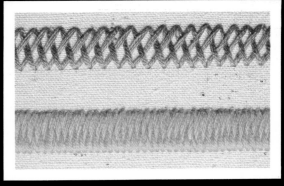

● BASKET STITCH

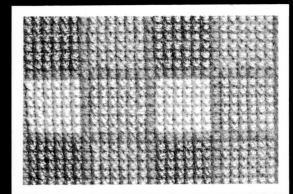

● CROSS STITCH

● CROSS STITCH — ALTERNATE

● CROSS STITCH — DIAGONAL

CROSS STITCH ● Victorian panel in wool framed as a picture

This chapter contains descriptions, diagrams and stitched samples of thirty-four crossed stitches, and six other embroidery stitches which can be used in conjunction with them. A crossed stitch is one that is formed by two or more stitches crossing each other. The angle of crossing can vary from the right angle of simple cross stitch to the oblique angle of herringbone stitch. The stitches range from easy-to-work cross stitch through to the complicated, interlaced Maltese cross, which requires more expertise. They are arranged alphabetically in families. A cross-referenced section at the end of the chapter lists the stitches which are suitable for working on canvas, even-weave or common-weave fabrics.

■ EVEN-WEAVE

□ COMMON-WEAVE

■ CANVAS

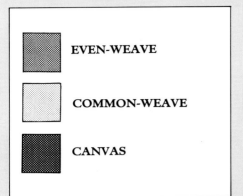

BASKET STITCH

Basket stitch produces a plaited effect and is useful for both fillings and edgings. It can be worked to give an open or closed finish and is used on common-weave fabrics. It is a close stitch, worked with a forward and backward motion.

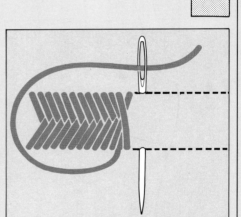

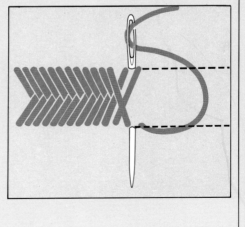

CROSS STITCH — also known as sampler stitch

Cross stitch is one of the best known of all embroidery stitches and is easy to work. It is extremely versatile, excellent for outlines, solid fillings, motifs and borders. The top diagonals should always be worked in the same direction, unless a deliberate light and shade effect is required, in which case their direction can be varied to catch the light.

Cross stitches can be worked individually, that is, a complete cross is worked before proceeding to the next one. This method produces neat, raised crosses. Cross stitch on canvas should always be worked in this way, on Penelope canvas for the best results. It is essential that each cross stitch completely covers the canvas, so choice of thread is important.

Cross stitch can also be worked in rows, a method particularly suitable for plain- and even-weave fabrics. A line of diagonal stitches is worked in one direction and then covered on the second journey by a line worked in the other direction.

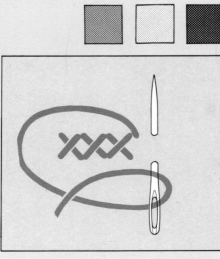

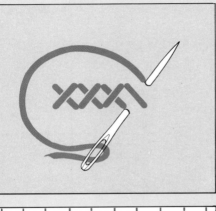

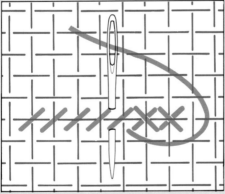

Cross stitch can also be worked in different combinations of half and threequarter stitches as shown below.

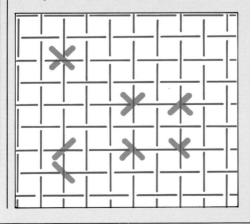

CROSS STITCH — ALTERNATE

This method of working cross stitch is suitable only for even-weave fabrics and will ensure a uniform tension and finish, particularly important when covering large areas. The lower row of diagonals is worked in two journeys and then the whole crosses are filled in alternately on two more journeys.

CROSS STITCH — DIAGONAL

Diagonal cross stitch is a canvas stitch worked diagonally from bottom right to top left. It is used as a filling stitch and each row can be worked in a different color to give a diagonally striped effect.

CROSS STITCH — DOUBLE — also known as double straight cross stitch

This is a canvas stitch consisting of a large upright cross overstitched by a smaller cross. It forms raised diamonds and is usually worked over four vertical and four horizontal canvas threads. Work the rows from left to right and then right to left.

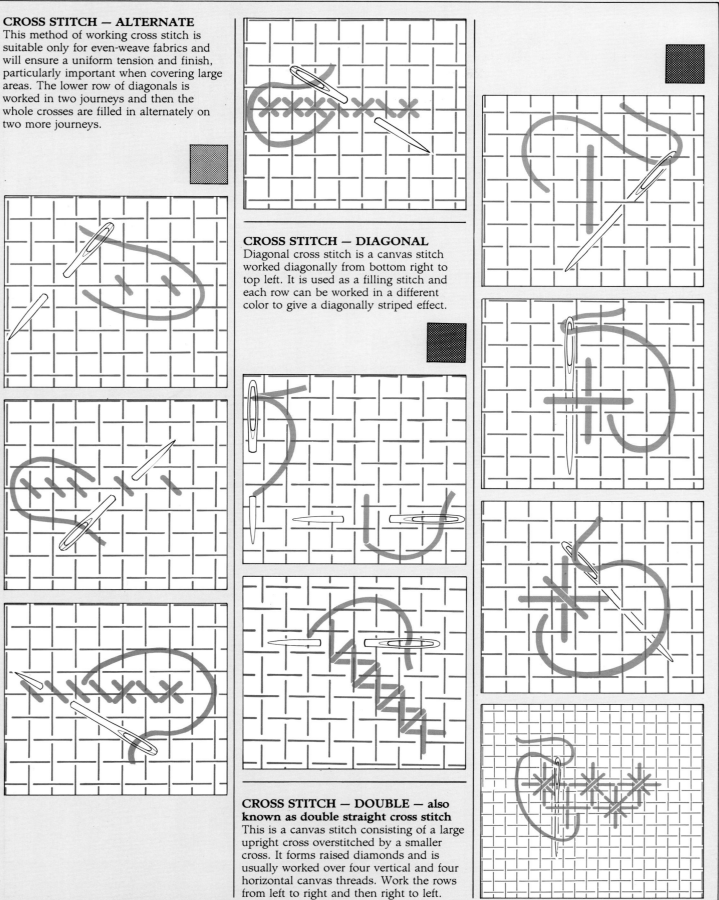

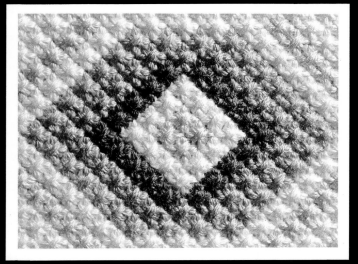

● CROSS STITCH — DOUBLE

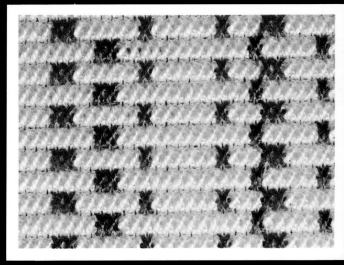

● CROSS STITCH — OBLONG

● CROSS STITCH — DOUBLE SIDED

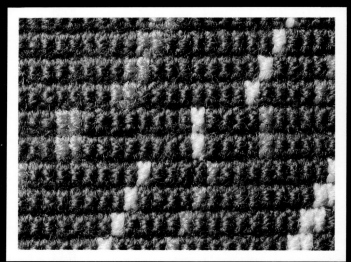

● CROSS STITCH — OBLONG WITH
 BACK STITCH

● CROSS STITCH — LONG ARMED

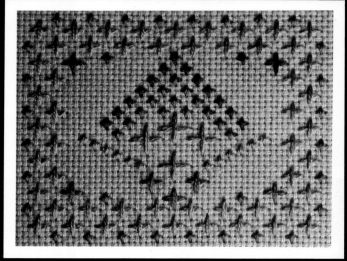

● CROSS STITCH — ST GEORGE

LONG ARMED STITCH ● seventeenth-century Italian border in silk on linen

CROSS STITCH — DOUBLE SIDED

Double sided cross stitch makes an identical stitch on both sides of the fabric and is used on common- and even-weave fabrics. It is an ideal form for fine, semi-transparent fabrics and for work which is reversible. Four journeys are needed to complete a single row, with half diagonals being worked at the end of the first journey and before the last (step 1 and step 5). The dotted lines show the stitches being made on the reverse side of the fabric. If it is necessary to re-cross a fully-made stitch to get to a point of continuation, this should be done as neatly as possible.

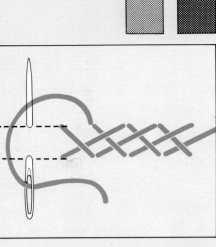

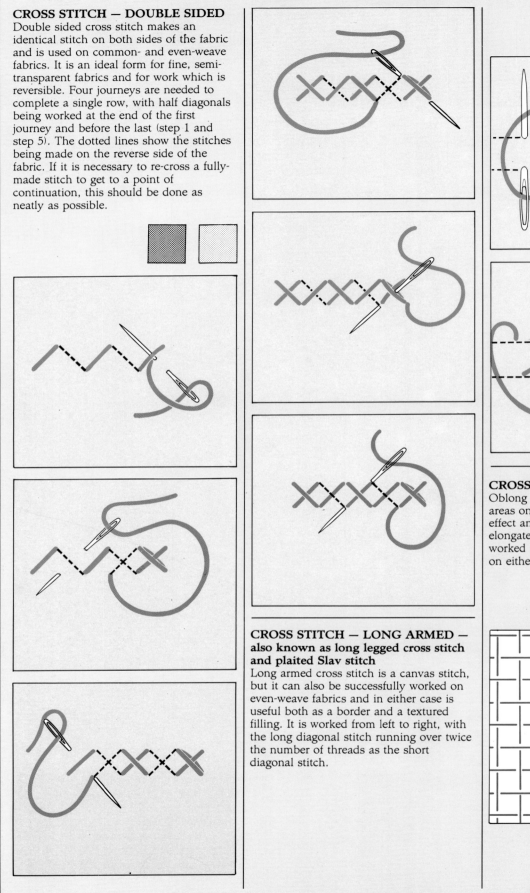

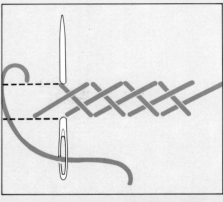

CROSS STITCH — LONG ARMED — also known as long legged cross stitch and plaited Slav stitch

Long armed cross stitch is a canvas stitch, but it can also be successfully worked on even-weave fabrics and in either case is useful both as a border and a textured filling. It is worked from left to right, with the long diagonal stitch running over twice the number of threads as the short diagonal stitch.

CROSS STITCH — OBLONG

Oblong cross stitch is used for filling large areas on canvas as it creates a neat, ridged effect and is quick to work. It is an elongated version of the basic cross stitch worked in rows rather than individually, on either mono or Penelope canvas.

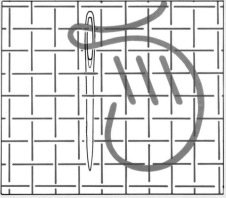

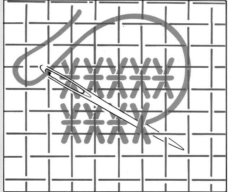

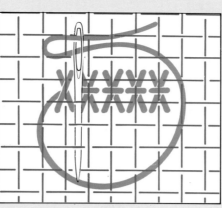

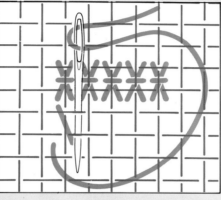

CROSS STITCH — OBLONG WITH BACK STITCH

This canvas stitch is very similar to oblong cross stitch, but gives a more crunchy texture over a large area. It is slower to work, as each cross is formed individually, with a back stitch across the center. The rows can be worked in either direction and mono canvas should be used.

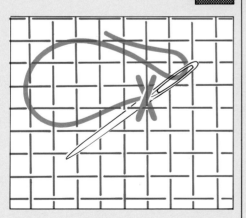

CROSS STITCH — ST GEORGE

This is an upright cross stitch used on common- and even-weave fabrics. It is mainly used as a filling stitch, and the density can be varied by altering the spaces between each cross. It is worked as a row of horizontal stitches which are then crossed by vertical stitches of the same length.

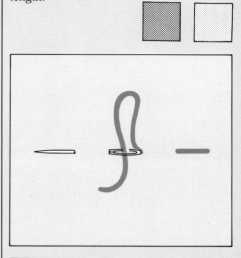

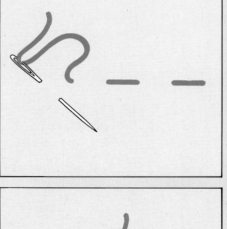

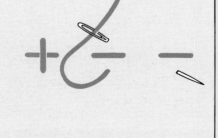

● ERMINE STITCH

● FLAT STITCH

● HERRINGBONE STITCH

● FERN STITCH

● FISHBONE STITCH

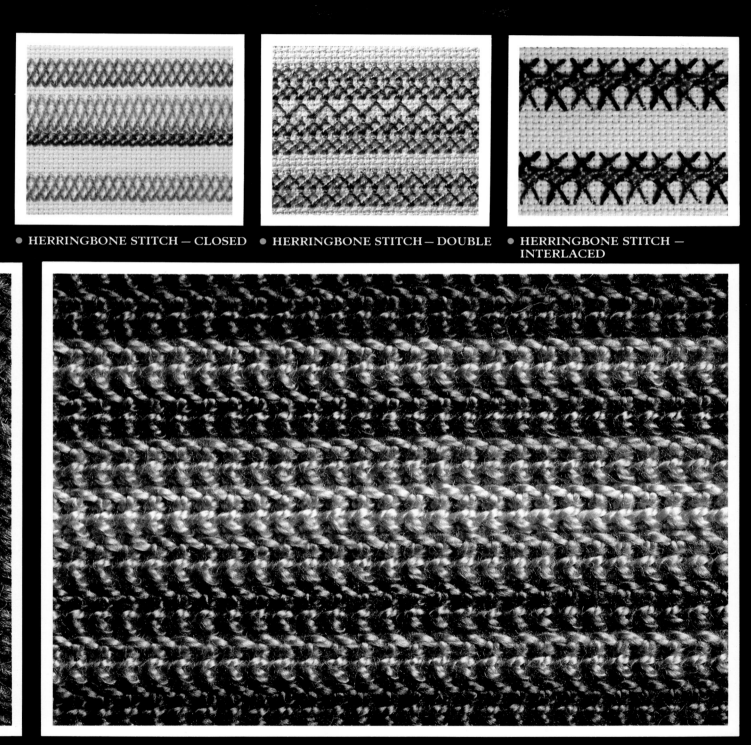

● HERRINGBONE STITCH — CLOSED   ● HERRINGBONE STITCH — DOUBLE   ● HERRINGBONE STITCH — INTERLACED

● GREEK STITCH

ERMINE STITCH

Ermine stitch is used on common-weave fabrics for fillings and borders. Its name comes from the ermine tail effect it makes when worked in black thread on a white background. It consists of a long vertical stitch which is then covered by an elongated cross stitch about one-third shorter. The cross should be placed above the base of the vertical stitch.

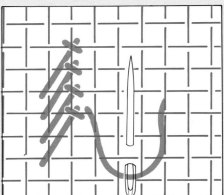

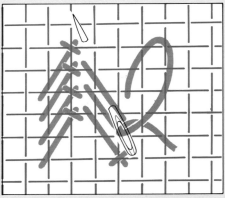

FISHBONE STITCH

Fishbone stitch makes an attractive chevron pattern and is worked on Penelope canvas. Each stitch consists of a long diagonal held down at one end by a short crossing stitch.

FERN STITCH

Fern stitch is a canvas stitch which forms plaited, vertical ridges and should be used on Penelope canvas. Each row of top-heavy crosses must be worked from the top to the bottom of the canvas.

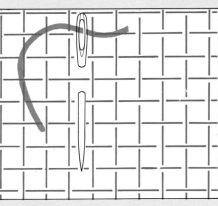

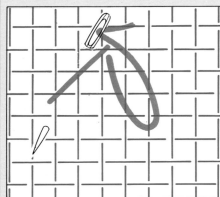

FLAT STITCH

Flat stitch is worked with a fairly thick thread on common-weave fabrics. It is used for filling small shapes solidly or can be worked in parallel rows to give a heavy outline to a shape. It is always worked from the inner margin to the outer margin.

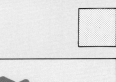

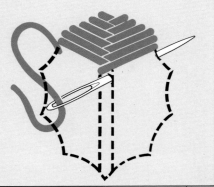

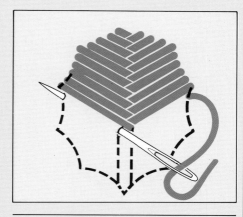

GREEK STITCH

Greek stitch is a canvas stitch which should be worked in a fairly coarse thread on either mono or Penelope canvas. It is similar to herringbone stitch, although the crosses are not spaced symmetrically, and it gives the effect of a plaited texture when applied over large areas.

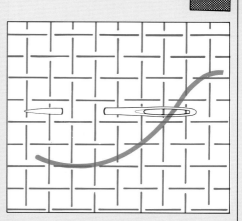

HERRINGBONE STITCH — also known as Russian stitch, Russian cross stitch or Mossoul stitch

Herringbone stitch is very simple and can be used on common- and even-weave fabrics and canvas. It can be worked in single rows or as a filling and it forms the foundation row for a number of more complicated stitches.

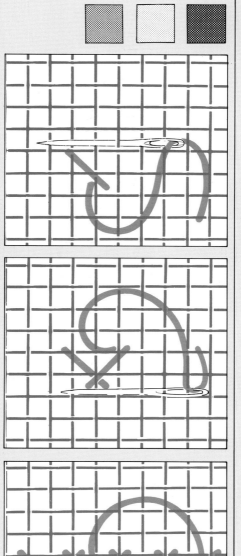

HERRINGBONE STITCH — CLOSED — also known as shadow stitch and double back stitch

Closed herringbone stitch can be used in two distinct ways. It can be worked on common- and even-weave fabrics as a border stitch to give a plaited effect. It is also used for shadow work on semi-transparent fabrics, with the rows of straight stitches appearing on the front of the work and the herringbone showing through the fabric in shadow form. It is worked in the same way as herringbone stitch, but the diagonals touch at the top and bottom.

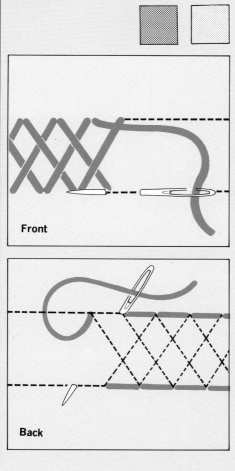

Front

Back

● HERRINGBONE STITCH —
  OVERLAPPING

● HERRINGBONE STITCH — TIED

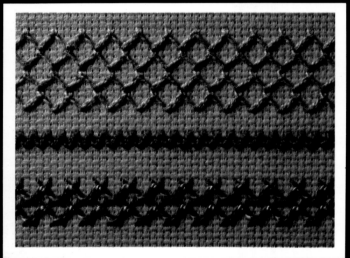

● HERRINGBONE STITCH —
  THREADED

● ITALIAN STITCH

● LEAF STITCH

● KNOTTED STITCH

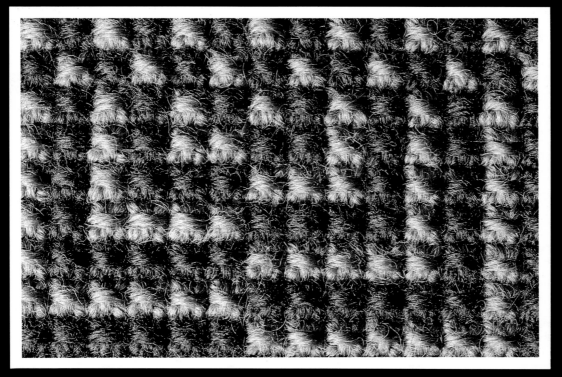

● LEVIATHAN STITCH

● **MALTESE CROSS**

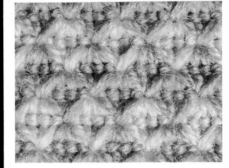

● **ROCOCO STITCH**

● **MONTENEGRIN STITCH**

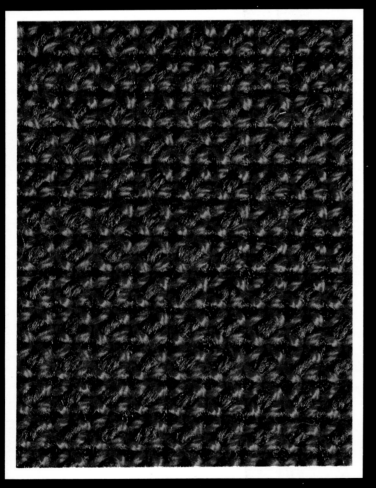

● **RICE STITCH**

● **LEVIATHAN STITCH — DOUBLE**

MONTENEGRIN STITCH ● **English sampler of 1656 in colored silks**

LEVIATHAN STITCH — DOUBLE

Double Leviathan stitch looks similar to the ordinary version but has a much heavier, crunchy appearance. It is slightly more complicated, and the sequence of stitches shown in the diagram must be carefully followed.

MALTESE CROSS — also known as Maltese Cross interlacing stitch

Maltese cross is an intricate laced stitch used on common- and even-weave fabrics. It can be worked as single motifs or as joined stitches to make a rich, heavy border. It is started by a framework of crossed stitches which must pass over and under each other in the sequence shown on the diagram. The interlacing will tighten them up, so work quite loosely at first to avoid puckering the fabric. This framework is then laced in a similar way to interlaced herringbone stitch, using either the same thread or one of a different color or texture. The motifs can be joined at the corners or placed edge to edge.

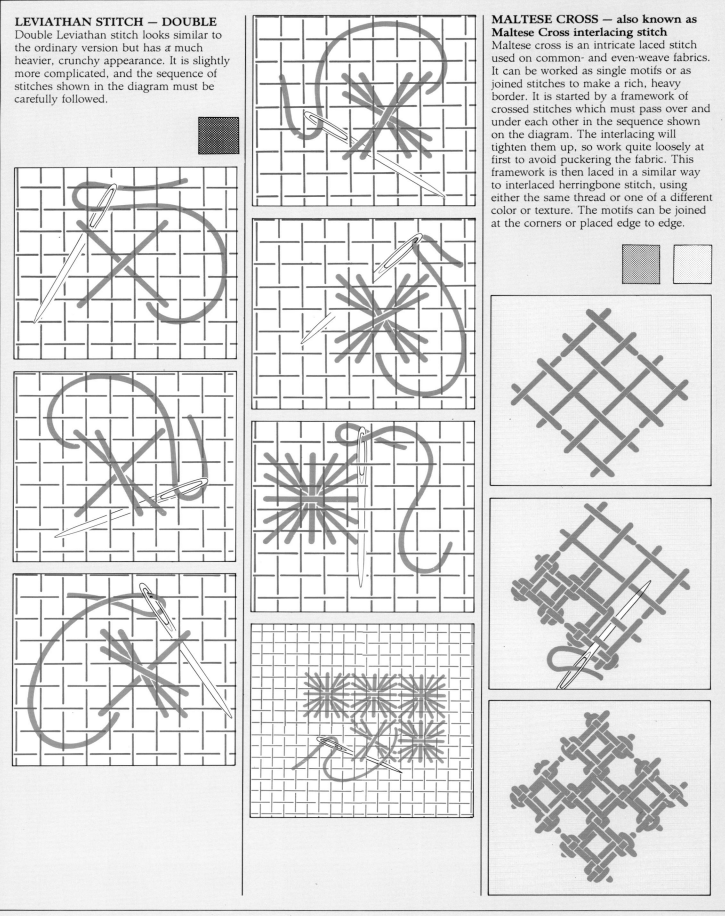

MONTENEGRIN STITCH

Montenegrin stitch is used on canvas and even-weave fabrics. The finished appearance is similar to long armed cross stitch with the addition of vertical bars. When this stitch is worked on canvas, a fairly coarse thread is necessary to cover the canvas completely.

RICE STITCH — also known as William and Mary stitch and crossed corners cross stitch

Rice stitch is a canvas stitch with a dense texture and, as it covers the canvas well, can be used for large areas. It can be worked in two colors or two thicknesses of thread by forming the large crosses first and then stitching the corner diagonals with a second thread. If using two thicknesses of thread, use the thickest thread for the large crosses and the thinner one for the corners. Interesting shaded effects can be achieved by working an area of large crosses in one color, and varying the colors of thread used for the corner stitches.

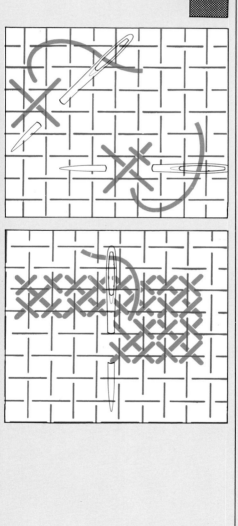

ROCOCO STITCH

Rococo stitch makes a dramatic background in needlepoint and should be worked on a wide mesh canvas with a fairly thick thread. It consists of four vertical stitches worked into the same space, tied down individually over one thread each with short crossing stitches. The vertical stitches curve when anchored into place on the canvas and make globe-shaped units.

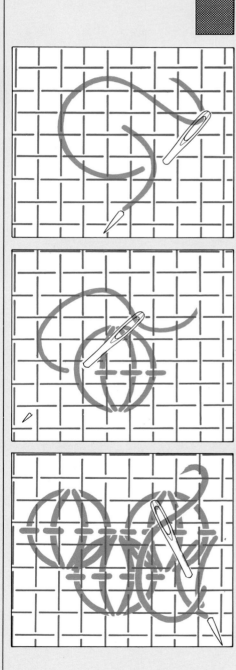

ROCOCO STITCH ● seventeenth-century English panel for a pincushion

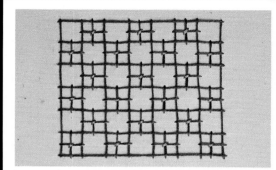

● **TOROCKO STITCH**

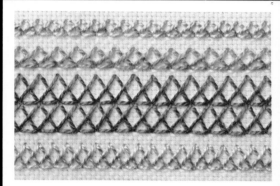

● **UNDERLINED STITCH**

● **VELVET STITCH**

● **BACK STITCH**

TOROCKO STITCH

Torocko stitch is a quickly worked filling stitch used only on common-weave fabrics. A foundation grid of evenly spaced long stitches is worked first, across the whole shape, and then covered with diagonal rows of upright crosses, with a short diagonal stitch worked from bottom left to top right to finish. The crosses can be worked in a different color from that used to form the grid, with a third color being used for the anchoring diagonal stitches.

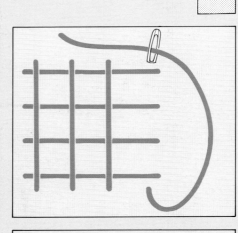

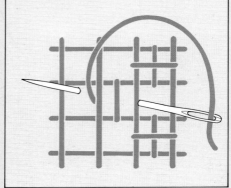

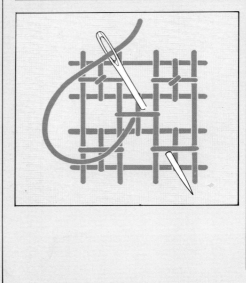

UNDERLINED STITCH

Underlined stitch is worked on canvas or even-weave fabrics. Each cross stitch is underlined by a horizontal straight stitch before the next cross is worked.

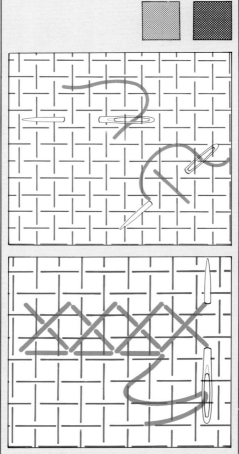

VELVET STITCH — also known as plush stitch

Velvet stitch resembles the pile of a carpet and is usually worked on Penelope canvas. Use a thick yarn or several strands of a fine yarn through the needle at the same time. The loops are cut and trimmed to length after all the stitching has been completed. If the stitches are worked very closely together on the canvas in thick yarn, the resulting pile will be dense enough to be sculptured into different levels with a sharp pair of scissors.

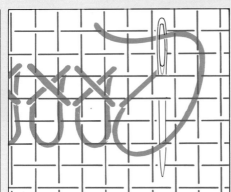

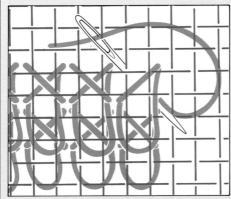

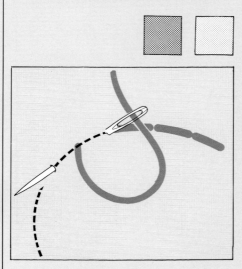

Other useful stitches

BACK STITCH — also known as point de sable stitch.

Back stitch is a slightly raised line stitch, worked from right to left on common- and even-weave fabrics. It should be kept small and even and looks rather like machine stitching. It is also used as a foundation for other stitches, such as Pekinese stitch.

FRENCH KNOT — also known as dot stitch and knotted stitch

French knots are a little tricky at first and are best worked on a frame, to leave both hands free for twisting the thread round the needle. They are used mainly on common-weave fabrics for powdering and sprinkling effects, or worked solidly where texture is required. French knots can also accentuate details and add highlights to solid areas of stitching on canvas.

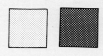

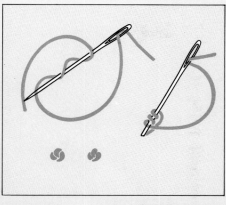

HOLBEIN STITCH — also known as double running stitch, stroke stitch and Romanian stitch

Holbein stitch is worked very simply and always on even-weave fabrics. A row of running stitch is worked first and on the return journey the spaces are filled in by a second row of the same stitch. This stitch is used in Assisi embroidery to outline the areas of cross stitch. It is similar to back stitch, but the finish is flat not raised.

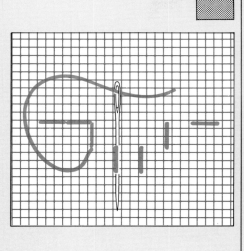

LONG AND SHORT STITCH — also known as plumage stitch and shading stitch

Long and short stitch is a variation of satin stitch that gives a gradually shaded effect. It is also used to fill an area which is too large or irregular to be covered neatly by satin stitch and can be worked on common- and even-weave fabrics and on canvas. The first row is made up of alternately long and short stitches which closely follow the outline of the shape to be filled. The subsequent rows are worked in satin stitches of equal length.

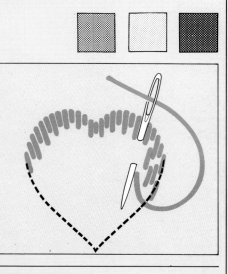

SATIN STITCH

Satin stitch appears easy, but some practice is required to work it neatly. The secret lies in making the stitches lie evenly and close together. It can be worked in varying lengths, but very long stitches may become loose and untidy. The stitches can be vertical or diagonal, with a change of direction giving the effect of light and shade. Satin stitch can be used on plain- and even-weave fabrics and on canvas, as outline or filling.

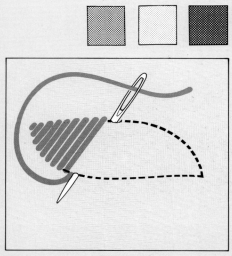

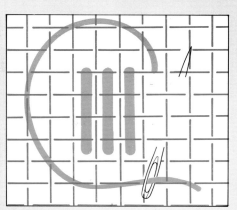

TENT STITCH — also known as petit point

Tent stitch is a canvas stitch used for fine work. It forms a small diagonal stitch which should always lie in the same direction. Tent stitch creates a flat, fairly smooth surface and combines well with heavier canvas stitches, accentuating their raised appearance.

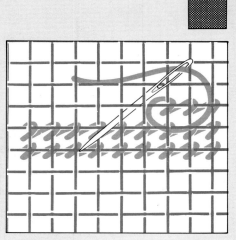

VELVET STITCH ● Victorian firescreen panel with cross stitch background

● SATIN STITCH

● FRENCH KNOT

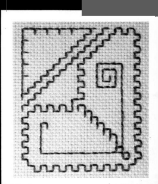

● HOLBEIN STITCH

● LONG AND SHORT STITCH

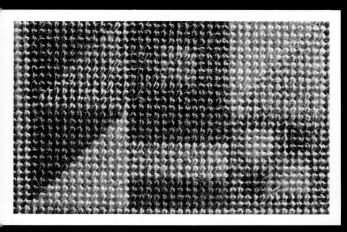

▶ TENT STITCH

Stitches for working on common-weave fabrics

Basket stitch
Cross stitch
Cross stitch — double sided
Cross stitch — St. George
Ermine stitch
Flat stitch
Herringbone stitch
Herringbone stitch — closed
Herringbone stitch — double
Herringbone stitch — interlaced
Herringbone stitch — overlapping
Herringbone stitch — threaded
Herringbone stitch — tied
Leaf stitch
Maltese cross
Torocko stitch

Back stitch
French knot
Long and short stitch
Satin stitch

Stitches for working on even-weave fabrics

Cross stitch
Cross stitch — alternate
Cross stitch — double sided
Cross stitch — long armed
Cross stitch — St. George
Herringbone stitch
Herringbone stitch — closed
Herringbone stitch — double
Herringbone stitch — interlaced
Herringbone stitch — threaded
Herringbone stitch — tied
Italian stitch
Leviathan stitch
Maltese cross
Montenegrin stitch
Underlined stitch

Back stitch
Holbein stitch
Long and short stitch
Satin stitch

Stitches for working on canvas

Cross stitch
Cross stitch — diagonal
Cross stitch — double
Cross stitch — long armed
Cross stitch — oblong
Cross stitch — oblong with back stitch
Fern stitch
Fishbone stitch
Greek stitch
Herringbone stitch
Herringbone stitch — double
Italian stitch
Knotted stitch
Leviathan stitch
Leviathan stitch — double
Montenegrin stitch
Rice stitch
Rococo stitch
Underlined stitch
Velvet stitch

Long and short stitch
Satin stitch
Tent stitch

The Projects

The projects in this section of the book have been designed to show some of the wide possibilities of the different types of cross stitch explained in the stitch directory. They range from small, quick-to-work items to more complicated and time-consuming projects suitable for someone already skilled in embroidery techniques. Projects for children's clothes and embroidered bedding are worked in cross stitch on gingham, ideal for giving the beginner confidence in handling fabric and threads. The most important thing to remember when selecting an item to make is to work within your capabilities at first and gain experience. Then you can move on to a more challenging project where a certain amount of technical skill is necessary to achieve a good finish to your work. Remember, too, to buy the best materials you can afford so that the finished item will last well.

It is hoped that experienced stitchers will use the projects to spark off new ideas for their own designs. For those less familiar with the materials and techniques, note that if you wish to substitute different fabrics and threads from those suggested in the project instructions it is always a good idea to work a small test piece on spare fabric or canvas first, to see what different effects can be achieved. With practice, you will soon know instinctively which stitches and threads to use to get exactly the result you want. Keep in mind that the amounts of thread you will need can vary considerably if different stitches are used. For example, a highly textured stitch, such as double leviathan stitch, can require twice as much thread as a flat, smooth stitch to cover the same area. Working a sample piece can help you calculate how much thread to buy. Simple devices such as changing the gauge of the fabric and the thickness of thread can alter a design dramatically and this is an interesting effect to explore.

Pillow covers ● 72

Key tags ● 78

Jumper ● 84

Baby's bib ● 76

Decorative gingham border ● 80

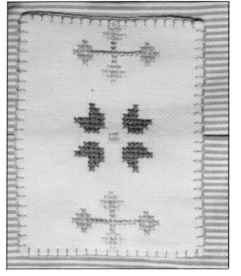

Overalls pocket and patches ● 85

Evening shirt ● 77

Pincushions ● 82

Landscape picture ● 86

Repeat pattern purse ● 87

Borders for bedlinen ● 92

Badges ● 95

Tablecloth and napkins ● 88

Lampshade border ● 90

Photograph frame ● 93

Gingham tablecloth ● 96

Border pattern belt ● 91

Blouse with net applique ● 94

Needlepoint chair seat ● 98

Striped panel pillow

The basic construction of this design is really quite simple, but the effect is very striking. A pattern of regular stripes is interrupted by small blocks shifted out of alignment or imposed diagonally and horizontally on the vertical pattern. To create an alternate design, varying the colors or widths of the stripes, paint stripes on paper and cut out small blocks, leaving a broad area of pattern. Arrange the blocks on the striped area, moving and turning the shapes until you arrive at a pleasing design. Trim the small pieces to shape as necessary and chart the full design on graph paper.

MATERIALS

Pillow form 12 in (30 cm) square
Penelope canvas, 10 gauge
Stranded floss 1 skein of each color
        silver grey
        charcoal grey
        royal blue
        black
Black tapestry yarn
Crewel and tapestry needles
Embroidery frame or stretcher
Heavy cotton or light wool backing fabric

METHOD

Copy the design on graph paper, charting one square of the graph to one woven block of canvas. The striped section is 5 in (12.5 cm) square and the panel is finished to the size of the pillow form by the wide border all around.

Stretch the canvas on the embroidery frame and baste the central lines. Work the striped panel from your chart, in cross stitch using six strands of floss. When the central design is complete, work the border in tapestry yarn. The border stitches are Leviathan stitch and oblong cross stitch with back stitch, alternating in double rows, up to the last eight rows, which are all oblong cross stitch with back stitch.

FINISHING

Finish the cover by the instructions given for the Landscape Picture Pillow above.

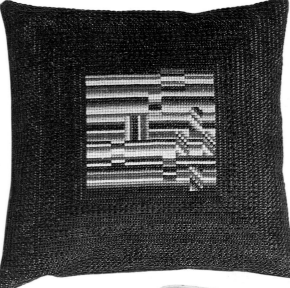

Checkerboard motif pillow

This pillow cover features 16 different geometric motifs, each set in a square of color to form a checkerboard pattern. The motifs are linked visually by the use of a limited color scheme. The design for the cushion cover differs from the previous two, in that the embroidered panel is mounted on a separately made fabric cover and finished with a braid trim, rather than forming one complete side of the cover.

The design can be interpreted in different ways by a simple change of scale. If the embroidery is worked on 14 gauge canvas instead of the 7 gauge used in the

original, and stitched in finer yarn, the complete design can be stitched four times in the same area, giving 64 motifs in all. Alternatively, it can be simplified: for example, by stitching alternate squares in a plain color and using only half the number of motifs.

MATERIALS

Pillow form 15 in (38 cm) square
Penelope canvas, 7 gauge
Tapestry yarn 5 skeins of each color
        white
        bright pink
        yellow ocher
        light brown
        1 skein of black
        2 skeins of dull
         mauve
Tapestry needle
Embroidery frame or stretcher
Heavy cotton or light wool fabric for the pillow cover
Braid
Cording
12 in (30 cm) zipper
Sewing needle and thread

METHOD

Work directly from the chart or copy the design onto graph paper. The finished area of stitching is just under 14 in (35 cm) square and you should allow a margin of 3 in (7.5 cm) of canvas all around. Stretch the canvas on the frame, baste the central lines and work the design from the chart, using cross stitch throughout.

FINISHING

Take the canvas off the frame and block it. When it is thoroughly dry, trim the margin to ½ in (1.5 cm) all around. This margin must be covered by the braid you have chosen to edge the design, so trim it more closely if necessary.

Cut two pieces of fabric 17½ in (44 cm) square, which includes seam allowances of 1¼ in (3 cm). On the right side of the piece, center the embroidery and pin it in place. Baste around the edge of the canvas, close to the stitching. Baste braid around the edge of the embroidery, covering the raw edges of the canvas and mitering the braid at each corner. Stitch the braid in place by hand or machine.

Make up the pillow cover as shown in the diagram on page 73, inserting cording in the seams and a zipper to close the opening. You can buy readymade cording, or make it up (see diagram) by covering piping cord with strips of the fabric used for the pillow cover. This method of finishing gives a more formal appearance and you can unzip the cover to remove the pillow form, but if you prefer a simpler method of finishing, omit the cording and follow the instructions given for the Landscape Picture Pillow.

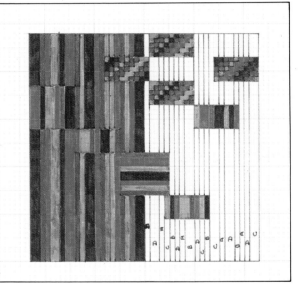

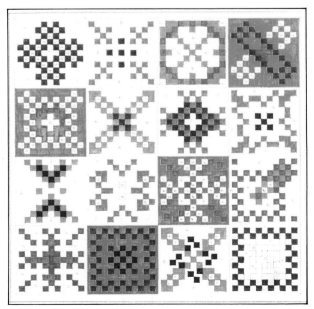

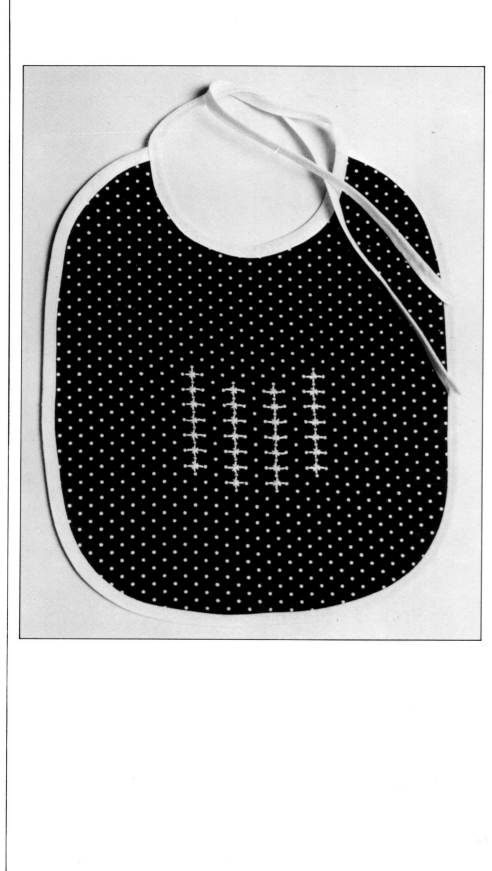

BABY'S BIB

The bib is made from a red fabric with small white polka dots, which form a regular 'grid' for placing the stitches. The design consists of double cross stitches placed between the dots. Choose a fabric with small, quite closely-spaced dots; otherwise the stitches become too large and are not so durable.

The design has been worked as four rows of double cross stitch concentrated at the center of the bib. It could easily be repeated right across the shape or worked down one side. The stitching is in white stranded floss; another variation on the design would be to work alternate stitches in different colors.

MATERIALS
Cotton fabric with polka dot pattern
Stranded floss 1 skein of white
Crewel needle
Embroidery hoop
Cotton or vinyl backing fabric
White bias binding

METHOD
Cut the polka dot fabric to size; the example shown is 9 in (23 cm) deep by 7½ in (19.5 cm) wide. Follow the charted design, working the double cross stitch with two strands of floss.

FINISHING
When the embroidery is complete, lightly press the fabric. Cut the backing fabric to the same size as the bib. Place bib and backing together and stitch or hand-sew binding around the outside edge. Finally, stitch bias binding around the neck edge, extending it on either side to make strings for tying the bib.

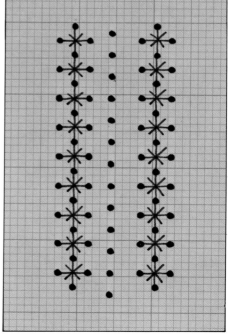

EVENING SHIRT

The evening shirt has a front panel of embossed diamond-pattern fabric which provides a grid for working the embroidery stitches. This facilitates regularity in the size and distribution of stitches and this type of decoration could be applied to any garment with a similar texture or pattern that provides a regular framework. In keeping with the formal style, the crossed stitches are worked in black and white thread on the white fabric.

MATERIALS

Evening shirt
Stranded floss 1 skein of each color
                  black
                  white
Crewel needle
Embroidery hoop

METHOD

The design consists of rows of double cross stitch in black, each stitch overworked with a single cross stitch in white. Start at the left side of the neck edge and work a vertical row of double cross stitch, using three strands of floss in the needle. When that is complete, work the next row approximately ¾ in (2 cm) from the first, placing it regularly on the diamond pattern of the fabric. Then work a white cross stitch over each of the black double cross stitches.

Repeat the design on the right side of the shirt, again working from the neck edge. Remember to make allowance for the width of the buttonhole tab when calculating where to place the stitches, and count the diamond shapes in the fabric carefully to make both sides the same.

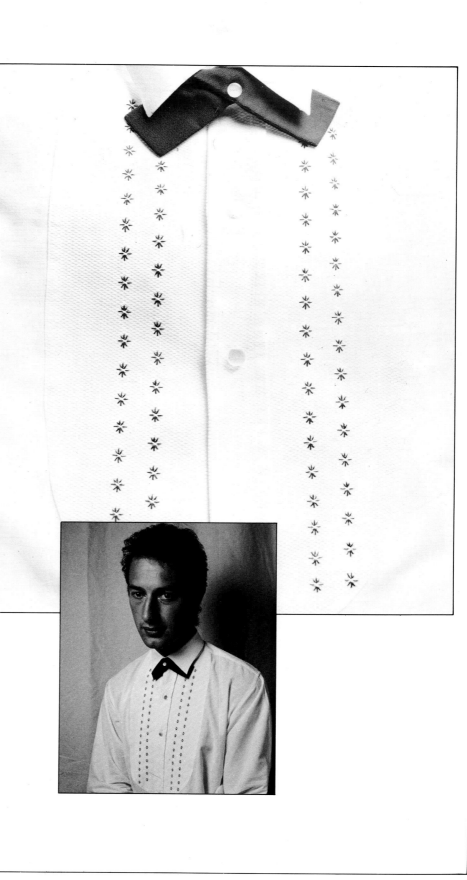

KEY TAGS

Small items such as these two key tags are quick to work and ideal for using up scraps of canvas and thread. The tags are worked on rigid plastic canvas, which can be held in the hand rather than on a frame while you are stitching and has the added advantage of not requiring stiffening. In these examples the front and back are worked separately and the design appears only on one side. Design problems are simplified in such a small area and a project on this scale is a useful vehicle for trying new motifs and fancy stitches.

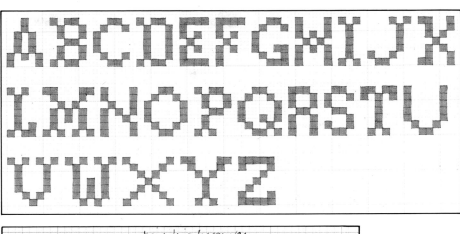

Monogram key tag

To make a personalized key tag, select your initial from the alphabet given here, look through the book for a different letter style, or chart one to your own design. NOTE that the letters in the alphabet have different widths. If your own initial is a wider letter than the J shown here — M or O, for example — you may need to broaden the shape of the whole tag to accommodate the design. You could, alternatively, develop a monogram using two or more initials, insert a tiny floral motif, or edge the design with a border.

MATERIALS

Plastic canvas, 10 gauge
Tapestry yarn   1 skein of cream
                scraps of scarlet, bright
                pink and purple
Tapestry needle
Metal split ring

METHOD

Work the front and back of the tag following the chart. The initial is worked in rice stitch, otherwise tent stitch is used throughout. Do not press the finished embroidery as a warm iron will damage the plastic canvas.

FINISHING

Trim the canvas close to the stitching, as shown by the trim line on the chart. Place the two pieces wrong sides together and stitch the edges together with overcast stitch (see diagram). Thread the split ring through the top.

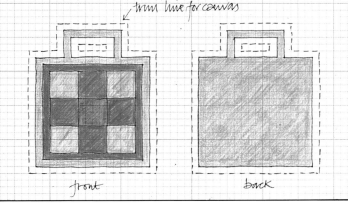

Nine-stitch key tag

The basic checkerboard pattern of this design is enlivened by the heavy texture of double Leviathan stitch. The monochrome color scheme enhances the contrast between the raised center and the flat area of tent stitch surrounding it. A strong contrast — white or a very pale color against a clear, bright hue — could also prove effective if you want to accentuate the inner squares.

MATERIALS

Plastic canvas, 10 gauge
Tapestry yarn   1 skein of light blue
                scraps of royal blue and
                turquoise
Tapestry needle
Metal split ring

METHOD

Work the front and back of the tag separately, using double Leviathan stitch to make the blocks and tent stitch for the border and the plain back. Do not press the finished work.

FINISHING

Make up and neaten the tag with overcast stitch, as described above.

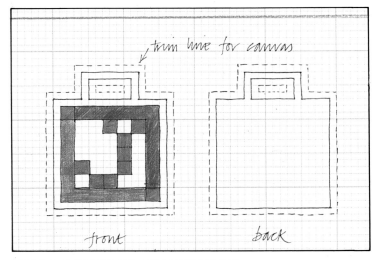

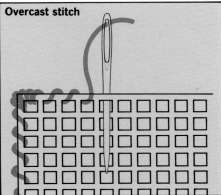

Overcast stitch

79

DECORATIVE GINGHAM BORDER

This border has been designed to show how the check grid of gingham fabric can be changed very effectively by careful use of colors. The stitching is quite simple — a large Leviathan stitch is worked over each square on the fabric and then each of these stitches is overworked with a small cross stitch. It is the use of the three colors which creates the design, by making the checks distort into stripes. The illusion is created by careful distribution of tones; if you are working on red gingham, for example, the color scheme might be red, white and green, corresponding to the black, white and red used here.

In this project, the border is applied to an easy-to-make summer skirt, but the design would also be suitable for kitchen curtains. Or you can adapt the sewing instructions to make a pretty apron, adding a waistband, ties and a pocket to the fabric.

MATERIALS

Black and white gingham with checks ¼ in (1 cm) square
Stranded floss 6 skeins of scarlet
　　　　　　　8 skeins of white
　　　　　　　10 skeins of black
Elastic ½ in (1.5 cm) in width
Sewing needle and thread.

METHOD

The skirt is simply made, with a center back seam and elasticized waist, from a rectangle of fabric. Cut the gingham to a rectangle with the long side measuring about three times your waist size and the short side allowing for the length of skirt you prefer, plus 4 in (10 cm) for the hem and 2 in (5 cm) for the elastic casing.

Following the chart, work the embroidery along one long side of the rectangle, placing the bottom row of stitching 5 in (12.5 cm) from the raw edge of the fabric. Use three strands of floss. Make sure that the embroidery finishes at either end on checks that will match the pattern when the skirt is finished.

FINISHING

Press the embroidered border lightly. Make a 1 in (2.5 cm) flat seam at the back of the skirt and turn up 4 in (10 cm) at the bottom for the hem. Handsew the hem and press it carefully.

Turn in 2 in (5 cm) of fabric at the top of the skirt and stitch all around by machine, 1 in (2.5 cm) below the fold. Make a second row of stitching ¾ in (2 cm) below the first, leaving a small gap near the back seam where you can thread the elastic into the casing. Insert the elastic and adjust it to your waist size; sew the ends together securely. Close the gap in the casing and give the skirt a final press.

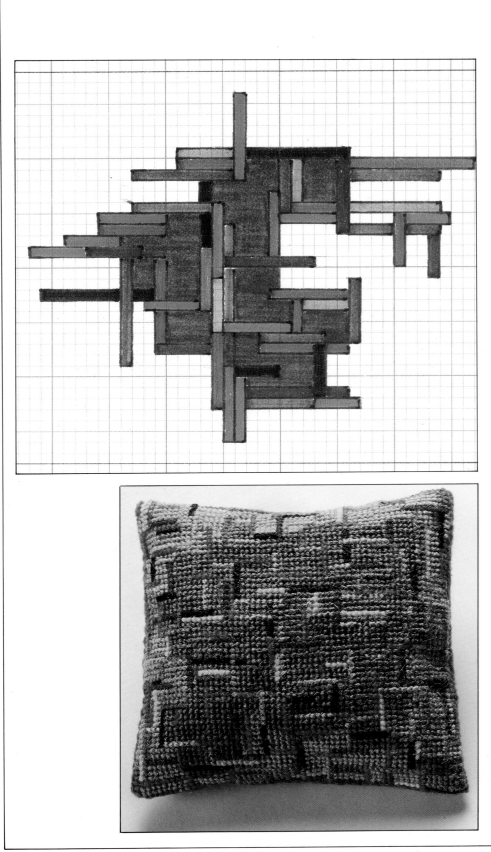

PINCUSHIONS

Small pincushions are invariably useful to stitchers and embroiderers and they make delightful gifts or bazaar items. From the technical viewpoint, they have the advantage of being quick to work, so you can not only practice good stitching, but also use the small format to try out different ideas on design and color that can be translated into larger projects such as bags, chair seats or full size pillows. The designs shown here indicate the variety that can be achieved with simple blocks or lines of stitching. You could also work out floral motifs, snowflake designs, stylized animals or sections of border patterns.

Crazywork pincushion

This pincushion was designed to use up small lengths of colored threads left over from other projects. In this case all the threads are tapestry yarns, but you could substitute knitting worsted or textured yarns. To accommodate thick or nubby yarns, you should use a more open-weave canvas than that given in the list of materials.

The design was developed by working at random over the canvas, a free approach that even the most inexperienced stitcher can use confidently on this scale. The bright colors were embroidered first and the remaining areas of canvas blocked in afterward — light grey around the edges and darker grey in the middle, but the background could be a single color if preferred. You can select any combination of colors, but this type of design is most effective when strong colors are worked first and neutral tones or low key colors used to fill the background.

MATERIALS

Mono canvas, 14 gauge
Tapestry yarn
       Left-over lengths or part skeins

light grey	green
dark grey	red
black	light blue
yellow	medium blue

Tapestry needle
Felt square for backing
Kapok or other stuffing
Sewing needle and thread

METHOD

The pincushion is 5 in (12.5 cm) square and the embroidery is worked entirely in cross stitch. The chart shows the central section of the pincushion, which you can use as a guide to the whole design. Work the bright colors first, starting at the center and working outward. When you have distributed a selection of colors all over the surface, block in the remaining areas of canvas.

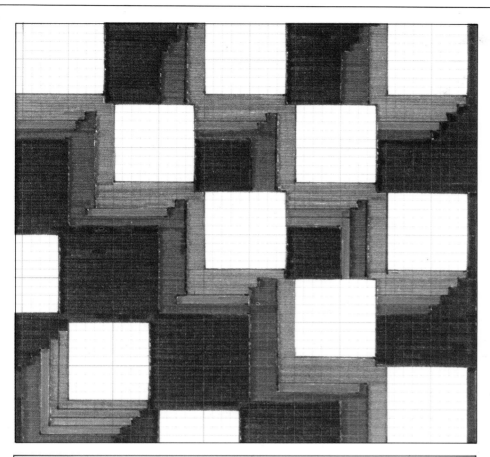

Block pattern pincushion

This is a bold and unusual design, carefully devised to create a three-dimensional effect. The strong contrast between black and white is pointed up by the use of close tones of grey and blue; the design would be changed considerably if the tonal contrasts were interpreted in vivid colors such as red and green.

MATERIALS

Mono canvas, 12 gauge
Tapestry yarn   1 skein of each color
               black
               white
               silver grey
               light blue
               grey-blue
Tapestry needle
Felt square for backing
Kapok or other stuffing
Sewing needle and thread

METHOD

The pincushion is 5 in (12.5 cm) square and the design is worked in cross stitch. Each square on the chart represents one woven square of the canvas. Start by stitching a block of color at the center of the design and then work outward, following the chart.

FINISHING

(both pincushions)
Trim the edges of the canvas to a margin of ½ in (1.5 cm) all around the design. Turn back the edges and miter the corners (see page 91). Stitch the felt square to three sides of the cross stitch square. Fill the pincushion with the stuffing, packing it tightly into the corners and padding the shape evenly. Stitch the canvas and backing fabric together along the fourth side.

JUMPER

A simple pattern for a child's jumper includes a flat yoke and patch pockets, which are ideal features for decorative stitching. Gingham or polka dot fabrics provide a grid for stitching, so there is no need to transfer the design to the fabric — you can work directly from charted motifs. The embroidery is worked before the dress is assembled, and each piece of fabric can be conveniently held in a hoop to facilitate neat stitching. You can adapt the idea of letters, numbers and a stylized bird motif, to develop a personalized design for your child — for example, the child's initials and age, a motif representing a favorite animal and so on.

MATERIALS

Jumper pattern
Gingham, with small checks, in pale blue
Stranded floss 1 skein of bright red
　　　　　　　　scraps of bright
　　　　　　　　　　　　blue
Crewel needle
Embroidery hoop

METHOD

Cut out the pieces of the dress, following the pattern. Stretch the yoke section in the embroidery hoop and follow the charted design, working cross stitch with three strands of floss. Work motifs on the pockets in the same way.

FINISHING

Lightly press the embroidered sections and make up the dress according to the pattern instructions.

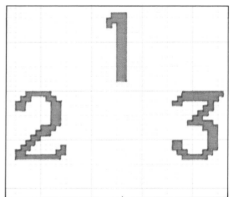

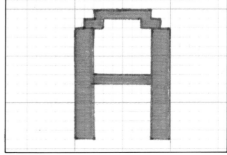

OVERALLS POCKET AND PATCHES

To decorate clothing in a fabric which is too tightly woven, plain or irregularly patterned to accommodate direct stitching, you can add patch pockets and knee patches made of a suitable even-weave fabric that provides a stitching grid. These pink and white cotton overalls are brightened up with patches of white Hardanger stitched with floral motifs in pink and green. You can apply the same principle to overalls or a jumper made in denim, canvas or corduroy, choosing different motifs and colors to suit the style. To add to the effect, the patches are sewn to the garment with a decorative edging stitch.

MATERIALS

Overalls
Hardanger even-weave fabric, 24 gauge, in white
Stranded floss   1 skein of each color
                 pale pink
                 rose pink
                 cerise pink
                 pale green
Crewel needle
Embroidery hoop

METHOD

In these examples the pocket measures 4¼ x 3 in (11 x 8 cm) and the patches 2½ x 3 in (6.5 x 7.5 cm). The pocket is made from a double layer of fabric. Work the embroidery in a hoop, using two strands of floss. Then cut a rectangle of fabric twice the length of the pocket, with the motifs centered on half the area. The patches are made from a single layer of fabric, so cut the exact shape required after cross stitching the motifs.

FINISHING

To apply the pocket, fold the rectangle of fabric in half and turn in the raw edges, then pin it to the center front of the overalls, placing the folded edge at the top. Edge three sides of the pocket, and at the same time stitch through the fabric of the overalls, with blanket stitch (see diagram), using two strands of floss. Finish the top edge with blanket stitch, without sewing through the garment. Apply the knee patches in the same way, but stitch them down on all four sides.

An anchor motif is a popular choice for denim clothing. This example is simply worked in cross stitch, with red and blue cottons on even-weave fabric.

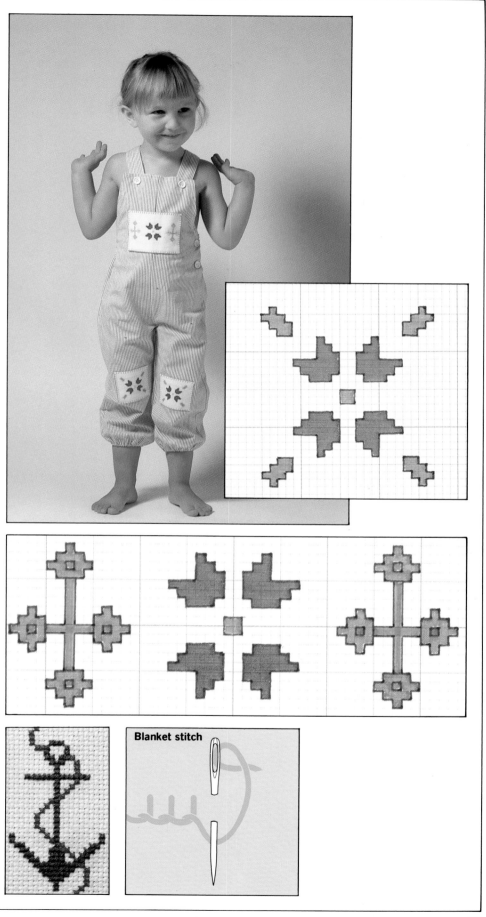

Blanket stitch

LANDSCAPE PICTURE

A picture designed with simple, stylized shapes provides a good base for experimenting with different textures in the threads and stitches. This example is quite small — 6 in (15 cm) square — and, on a limited scale, the simpler the design outlines, the better the result. The stitches have been chosen to contrast raised, heavily textured areas with flat, smooth shapes. Landscape is a suitable subject as it can be reduced to basic areas of color and texture.

MATERIALS

Mono canvas, 18 gauge
Stranded floss 1 skein of each color
        grey-green
        yellow-green
        dark moss green
        light brown
        tan
        scraps in a variety of
          blues
Pearl cotton no.8 scraps of bright rust
Pearl cotton no.5 1 skein of sky blue
        scraps of olive green,
        pale apple green,
        grey-green, bottle green,
        emerald, blue-green
Persian yarn scraps of grass green and
        light moss green
Tapestry needles
Waterproof ink
Fine paintbrush

METHOD

The finished picture measures 6 in (15 cm) square and you should allow a 5 in (12.5 cm) margin all around to facilitate blocking and mounting.

Trace off the design and square it up to the correct size. Transfer the design to the canvas, painting the outlines with waterproof ink and a fine brush.

Stretch the canvas in a frame and work each area, following the stitch and color key from the diagram. Use the stranded floss at the full thickness of six strands unless otherwise indicated. The stitches are cross, tent, knotted, fern, slanting satin stitch, double cross, Leviathan and double Leviathan. When working the larger stitches, you will find that at the outer edges of the shape, there is not always enough space left for a full stitch. Fill in these small areas with tent stitch in the appropriate color.

FINISHING

When the picture is completed, block the embroidery with the right side upward so the textured stitches will not be crushed. Allow it to dry thoroughly before mounting and framing the piece. The original picture has a simple, waxed wooden frame, to give a neat finish without distracting attention from the embroidery.

Key to stitch diagram *(right)*
1 Tent stitch
2 Knotted stitch
3 Double cross stitch
4 Satin stitch
5 Double Leviathan stitch
6 Leviathan stitch in two colors
7 Long armed cross stitch
8 Oblong cross stitch with back stitch
9 Fern stitch in two colors
10 Cross stitch

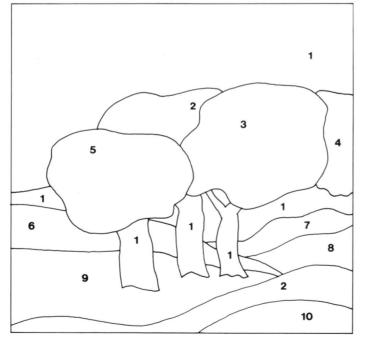

REPEAT PATTERN PURSE

This purse is made from a long rectangle of canvas, folded into three to form the two sides and the flap. Each section has the same geometric design, so all you need do is follow the chart and repeat the pattern three times. You require basic sewing skills to complete the project: the purse is given a neat finish with a lining, cord edging and a button fastening.

The choice of colors is a personal one and you can quickly trace off the design and try out different color combinations on paper, using paint or felt-tip pens. By repeating the design blocks side by side as well as vertically, you can adapt the idea to a larger purse or evening bag, following the same procedure for assembling. To add a glittering touch, consider using metallic threads or beadwork to decorate some of the shapes.

MATERIALS

Penelope canvas, 10 gauge
Tapestry yarn 1 skein of each color
              dark blue
              royal blue
              pale blue
              pink
              lilac
Tapestry needle
Lining fabric
Thin cord in dark blue
Button
Sewing needle and thread.

METHOD

The basic design is a rectangle 3 x 3½ in (7.5 x 9 cm), repeated three times to form a piece 9 x 3½ in (23 x 9 cm). Follow the chart, working cross stitch throughout. One square of the design corresponds to one woven square in the canvas.

FINISHING

Lay the finished piece flat and trim the canvas to leave a ½ in (1.5 cm) margin on each side. Turn in the edges over the back of the embroidery and miter the corners (see page 91).

Cut a piece of lining fabric slightly larger than the needlepoint and turn in the raw edges. Slipstitch the lining to the back of the embroidery.

Stitch cord all around the edge of the rectangle. At the center of one of the short sides of the rectangle, make a loop with the cord. This end of the fabric will form the purse flap and the cord loop will serve as a buttonhole. To finish the cord neatly, tuck the ends underneath the lining.

Fold the embroidery into three and stitch together two sections of the canvas on either side. Conceal the stitches as well as you can by working along the inner edge of the cord. Fold the flap down on the front of the purse and sew on a button to align with the loop of cord.

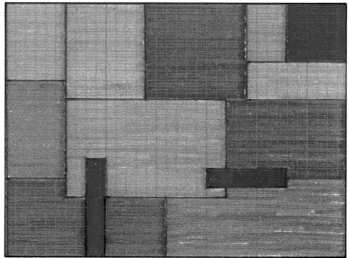

LAMPSHADE BORDER

A solid-colored lampshade is enlivened by an embroidered border, worked on plastic canvas and attached to the lower edge of the shade. It is made from four separate pieces joined together with braided cross stitch. As the plastic canvas is rigid you can cut the pieces to shape and there is no need to work on a frame. The border is designed for a lampshade which is square at the lower edge but you can easily adapt the idea for a rounded shade, and change the colors to suit the scheme of your furnishings.

MATERIALS

Lampshade, 8 in (20 cm) square at the lower edge
Plastic canvas, 9 gauge
Stranded floss 1 skein of each color
         light green
         olive green
         light pink
         dark pink
         grey-blue
Tapestry needle
Felt
Sewing needle and invisible thread

METHOD

Cut the plastic canvas into four strips 8 in (20 cm) wide and 1½ in (4 cm) deep. On each strip, cut indentations in the lower edge at every alternate group of four threads, to make the geometric design as shown. Trim the edges of the plastic to give the edging a smooth finish.

    Follow the charted design, using six strands of floss and cross stitch throughout. Each strip is bound at the top with braided cross stitch (see diagram) and finished at the lower edge with overcast stitch (see page 79), again using six strands of floss.

FINISHING

Cut strips of felt slightly smaller than the border sections and glue them to the back of the plastic canvas, using a latex glue. Leave to dry thoroughly.

    Join the four strips at the short ends with braided cross stitch. When the border is complete, attach it to the lower edge of the lampshade with small running stitches of invisible thread.

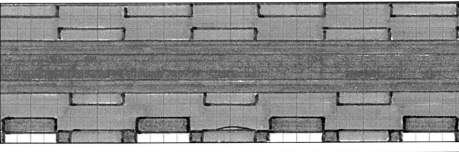

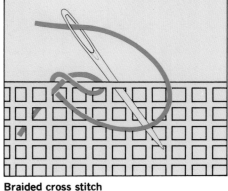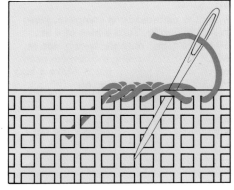

Braided cross stitch

BORDER PATTERN BELT

The design for this belt consists of a simple repeat pattern of interlocking L-shapes within a basic square. You can thus make the belt of a suitable length for your waist size by reworking the pattern as many times as is necessary. The blocks are bordered with heavy stripes which are also worked at each end of the belt to finish off the pattern. The colors used in the original design are close-toned, but the contrast created by setting a warm, bright rust against the clean blues and greens gives a rich, glowing effect. If you alter the colors, try to create a similar balance; you might choose a range of pastel hues to match a summer dress or dark, plummy tones for a winter outfit. Bright primary and secondary colors, as used in some styles of peasant embroidery, would make a striking accessory for a dress in black, white or a strong, plain color.

A simple strip pattern of this kind can be adapted to other accessories, such as a choker or wristband, or you could alternatively apply it to furnishings — as a bell pull or upholstery trimming, for example.

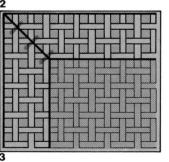

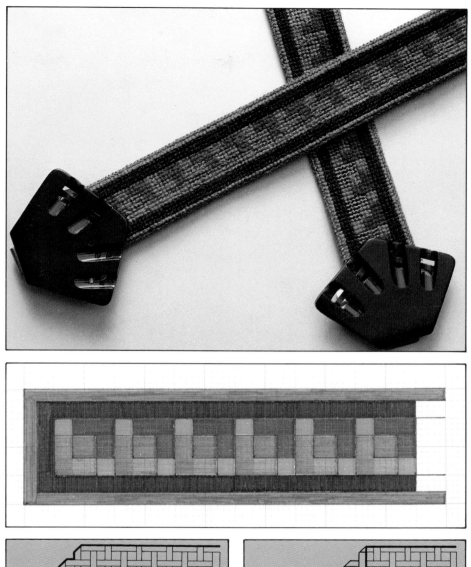

MATERIALS

Mono canvas, 18 gauge
Stranded floss 1 skein of each color
        black
        emerald green
        olive greeen
        royal blue
        rust
Crewel needle
Embroidery frame or stretcher
Belt buckle
Grosgrain ribbon or purchased belt stiffening
Sewing needle and thread

METHOD

The belt is just under 1¼ in (3 cm) wide but to avoid pulling the canvas out of shape as you work, stretch a broader section on a frame and trim it when the cross stitching is finished. Work cross stitch throughout with the needle threaded with three strands of floss. Follow the chart, working section by section until you have the required length.

FINISHING

Remove the canvas from the frame and trim it to within ½ in (1.5 cm) all around the stitched area. Turn in the raw edges and miter the corners (see diagram).

To attach the buckle, fold the end of the belt over the buckle bar and stitch the edges of the fold. Cut the ribbon or belt stiffening to the correct length and pin it to the wrong side of the belt. Secure it in place with small stitches along each edge.

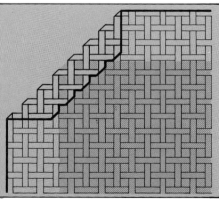

Mitering corners on canvas
1 Trim the corner of the surplus canvas to avoid excess bulk.
2 Turn over the cut canvas to the corner of the embroidery.
3 Fold in the side edges and stitch down the diagonal join, making sure the corner is square.

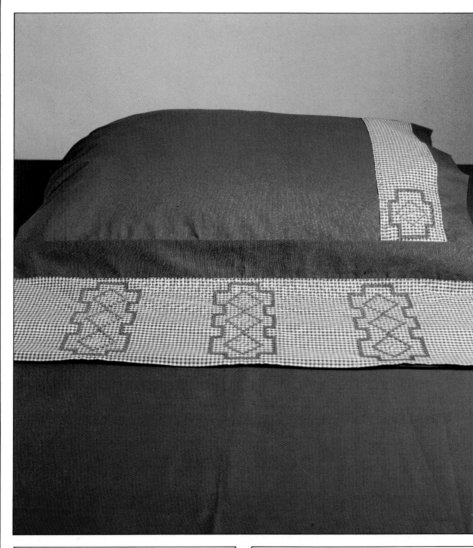

BORDERS FOR BEDLINEN

Embroidered gingham makes a decorative edging for a sheet and pillowcase. The cross stitch designs are repeated on strips of gingham — three centered pattern blocks for the sheet and two corner motifs for the pillow — which are sewn in place when the embroidery is complete. You can vary the design by repeating the motifs along the whole strip, or concentrating the embroidery at the corners of the sheet rather than at the center. The design can be used for a duvet cover or scaled down for a crib sheet and there are several attractive colors of gingham to choose from, to match different colored bedlinen. The embroidery colors consist of two shades closely related to the gingham and two which contrast, a balanced scheme which can be applied to other color ranges.

MATERIALS

Brown cotton sheet and pillowcase
Brown and white gingham
Stranded floss 1 skein of each color
               dark brown
               rust
               olive green
               deep yellow
Crewel needle
Sewing thread

METHOD

Measure the sheet and pillowcase and cut strips of gingham to fit across the width, to make a border 8½ in (21 cm) deep on the sheet and 4½ in (11 cm) deep on the pillowcase. These measurements can be adapted to your requirements, but make sure you can fit the cross stitch design comfortably within the strip. To avoid wasting fabric, you can cut shorter strips and stitch them together to the required length, making a neat seam with the gingham checks precisely matched.

Turn under and baste a hem of ½ in (1.5 cm) on either side of each strip. Find the center of the sheet border and stitch the first pattern block, using cross stitch and three strands of floss. In the charted design, one square of the grid is equivalent to one square of the gingham. Work the pattern block twice more, evenly spaced on either side of the central block. Work the smaller motifs at each end of the gingham strip cut to fit the pillowcase.

FINISHING

When the embroidery is complete, lightly press the strips of gingham with a warm iron. Stitch them by hand or machine to the sheet and pillowcase, leaving a border of plain fabric at the edge.

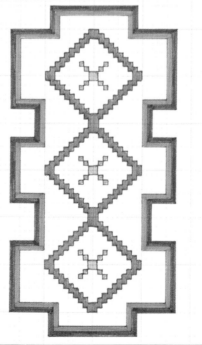

PHOTOGRAPH FRAME

A needlepoint border inside a cardboard mount makes an attractive and unusual frame for a photograph or small picture. The photograph and mount are sandwiched together inside a simple clip frame, inexpensive and easy to assemble, and are held in place by pressure from the glass and clips; there is no need to tape the photograph to the mount and you can remove it without damage to substitute another picture.

The border design makes use of a variety of stitches, including French knots, which are worked after completion of the canvas stitches. The design could be adapted to a number of photographs mounted together within a larger clip frame, with separate window mounts cut in the cardboard and edged with narrow borders of stitching.

MATERIALS

Clip frame
Mono canvas, 18 gauge
Stranded floss 1 skein of each color
          cream
          light blue
          medium blue
          bright pink
          pale green
Tapestry needle
Embroidery frame or stretcher
Mounting cardboard
Masking tape
Craft knife
Steel ruler

METHOD

The chart shows a section of the embroidery which you can convert to a full design of a suitable size for your photograph. Stretch the canvas on the frame and work the design using six strands of floss throughout. The stitches are long armed cross, double cross, tent and slanting satin. When the basic shape is complete, work the French knots over the upper section.

FINISHING

Block the embroidery face upward and allow it to dry thoroughly. With a very sharp pair of embroidery scissors, cut out the central portion of the canvas, trimming it close to the stitching. Trim the outside edges to a margin of ½ in (1.5 cm) around the design.

Cut a window in the cardboard mount to fit neatly around the outer edges of the embroidery. Trim the mount to the correct size for the clip frame and tape the embroidery inside the mount. Place the photograph on the backing board of the clip frame, put the mount over it and adjust them both to the correct positions; then cover them with the glass and put the clips in place.

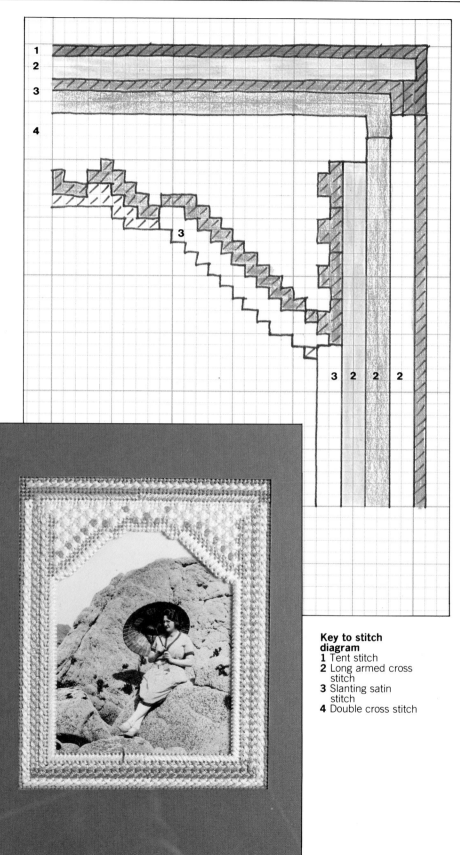

Key to stitch diagram
1 Tent stitch
2 Long armed cross stitch
3 Slanting satin stitch
4 Double cross stitch

BLOUSE WITH NET APPLIQUÉ

Fine net provides a perfect grid for cross stitch embroidery and is used here for decorative appliqué work on a silk blouse. The blouse is made up specially from a simple pattern, the appliqué stitched to the cut-out front of the blouse before the garment is assembled. This example is in raw silk, with silk embroidery and decorative beads on the net squares. For a cotton or polyester fabric, stranded floss would be a more suitable choice of thread. You could also apply embroidered net to a readymade blouse, providing the shape is suitable for this style of appliqué. You must be able to spread the blouse fabric easily in order to stitch the appliqué in place by machine.

MATERIALS

Blouse pattern
Raw silk fabric
Silk embroidery thread
    1 skein of each color
    pink
    green
    purple
Fine crewel needle
Embroidery hoop
Pink, purple and green net
Narrow ribbon in pink, green and purple
White pearl beads

METHOD

Cut the pattern pieces according to instructions. Cut the net into 2 in (5 cm) squares and arrange them on the front of the blouse, following the curve of the neckline. Baste them in place and then stitch along each edge by machine. Remove the basting thread.

All the embroidery stitches — cross stitch, double cross stitch and French knots — are worked with two strands of silk thread. Copy the designs shown in the photographs and add decoration with beads and bows when the stitching is complete.

FINISHING

Make up the blouse according to the pattern instructions.

The appliqué squares can be varied by working the same stitch patterns in different colors or changing the design in each square.

BADGES

The range of possible designs for a small badge or brooch is endless; any type of motif, lettering, geometric or stylized pattern can be worked out in different colors or textures of thread. Both these examples, one in tapestry yarn, the other in stranded floss, are stitched on plastic canvas. Since the canvas is rigid and does not fray, you can cut it to any shape and finish the edges with a binding stitch, such as the braided cross stitch used here.

Bird motif badge

MATERIALS

Plastic canvas
Tapestry yarns scraps of black, pink
and dark grey
Tapestry needle
Felt
Brooch pin or safety pin

METHOD

Cut the plastic canvas to shape, trimming the edges carefully to create a smooth finish. Following the charted design, work the motif in cross stitch and background in tent stitch. Finish the edges with braided cross stitch (see page 90).

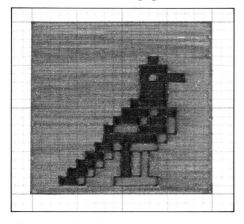

Geometric badge

MATERIALS

Plastic canvas
Stranded floss scraps of black and
white
Tapestry needle
Felt
Brooch pin or safety pin

METHOD

Cut the canvas to shape. Follow the design, working cross stitch with six strands of floss. Finish the edges with braided cross stitch.

FINISHING

(both badges)
Cut felt to the shape of the badge and glue it to the back of the canvas using glue suitable for fabrics. When the adhesive is completely dry, attach the pin to the felt backing.

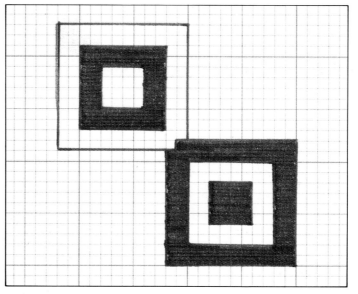

GINGHAM TABLECLOTH

Gingham checks provide an even grid for border patterns and the washable fabric makes an ideal cloth for a small table or will disguise, for example, a card table pressed into service for an informal buffet party. The border design can be extended to any length, to suit the dimensions of your table, and would work well on a different color of fabric. As in this example, an effective color scheme for the stitching consists of the basic colors of the gingham checks — black and white — and a single bright or contrasting color to highlight the design.

MATERIALS

Black and white gingham with ¼ in (1 cm) checks
Pearl cotton no.5, 4 skeins of black
                    2 skeins of
                    white
Coton à broder 2 skeins of yellow
Chenille needles
Sewing needle and thread

METHOD

Cut the gingham to size for the tablecloth, allowing 1½ in (4 cm) on each side for the hem. Work the design from the chart, placing the border 3¼ in (8 cm) from the edge of the fabric. For a tablecloth 33 in (84 cm) square, as shown, you will work the border motif ten times along each side The border is worked in cross stitch, the corner motifs combining ordinary cross with St George cross stitch. The gingham simplifies the stitching, as you work one stitch to one woven check.

FINISHING

When the embroidery is completed, press the fabric lightly. Turn in a double hem on each side of the cloth and handsew it neatly. Press the hem and work chevron stitch in yellow along the right side of the row of checks where the hemstitching is placed, to give a neat and decorative finish.

Chevron stitch

A pictorial motif *(above)* can be repeated to form a simple border pattern. Fine cross stitches in green and black on tiny red checks *(right)* trace a subtle border design with a featured motif at the corner.

Key to stitching chart

⊞	St George cross stitch in yellow
⊠	Cross stitch in yellow
⊠	Cross stitch in black
⊠	Cross stitch in white

Each square on the chart represents one square of the gingham check

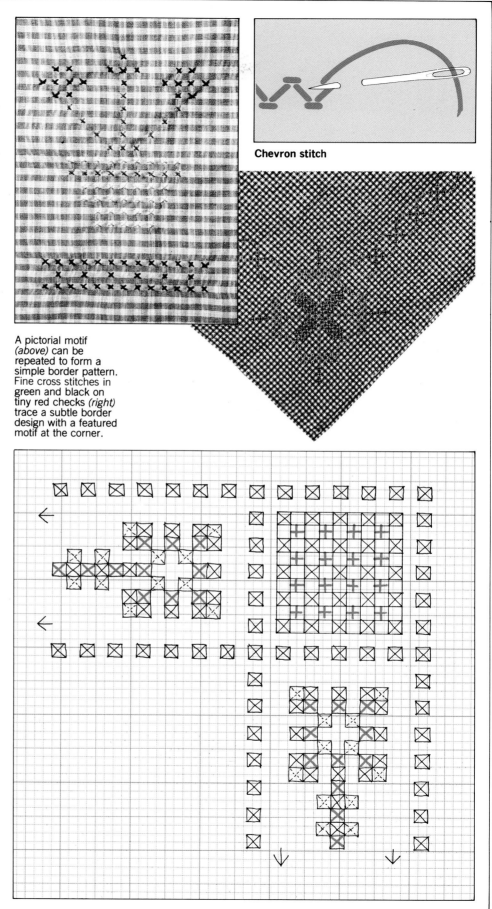

NEEDLEPOINT CHAIR SEAT

Needlepoint in tapestry yarn makes a suitable covering for chair seats as it is extremely hard-wearing and easy to mount on dining-chair seats, or on soft easy chairs. The chair shown here has a drop-in seat, which is the simplest type to attempt. In the following pages you will find different methods for seating a wood-frame chair with the needlepoint panel; alternatively, you can stitch it to the upholstery of a chair cushion, sofa back or footstool.

Many embroidery designs are suitable for upholstery, but small, all-over geometric designs and stripes are the most effective. They can be fitted to the tapering seat of a dining chair and even a simple geometric pattern offers plenty of scope for choosing attractive color combinations. Assuming that the chair is frequently in use, it is best to choose deep colors for the largest areas of stitching and highlight the design with paler tones.

To work out the design area for your chair seat, remove the original covering and measure the seat carefully. Allow an extra ½ in (1.5 cm) of embroidery all round, where the seat fits into the wood frame, to ensure that no canvas shows around the stitching. The materials below will serve as a guide, but you should work a small test piece on a spare section of canvas to calculate how much thread will be required for your particular project. It is always preferable to overestimate thread quantities for a large piece of needlepoint, as dye lots vary considerably and you may find it difficult to match the yarns if you run out.

Covering a chair seat

1 Strip any old upholstery from the chair seat, leaving the wood base and foam padding. Cover the foam with lining fabric, securing the lining with tacks on the underside of the seat. Pull the fabric over the corners and tack it.

2 Neaten each corner by folding in the fabric at either side. Crease it firmly with your fingers.

3 Push aside the folds and trim off the triangle of fabric underneath.

4 Put the folded sections back in place and hammer in tacks. If the folds are not neatly creased, press them with a damp cloth before tacking. Neaten all four corners in the same way.

5 Spread out the needlepoint face downward and place the chair seat on top, also right side down. Center it on the canvas and fold the edges of the needlepoint over the back of the frame. Secure the edges with tacks, working outward from the center of each edge and stretching the canvas gently into shape. Neaten the corners with folds, in the same way as for the lining fabric.

6 To finish off the underside of the seat, tack burlap across the wood frame. Stretch it evenly across the back of the seat and turn under the raw edges and corners neatly.

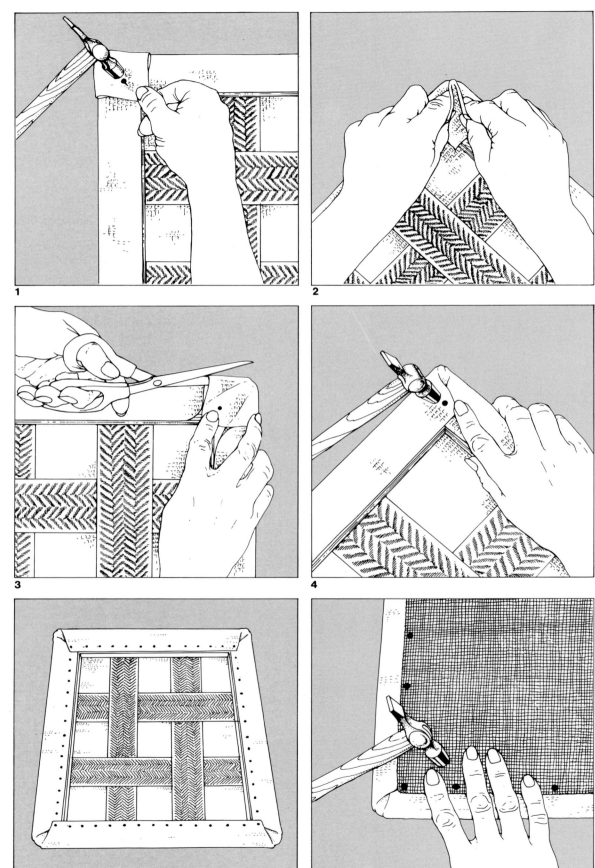

MATERIALS

Penelope canvas, 10 gauge
Tapestry yarns 6 skeins rust
               7 skeins light blue
               9 skeins medium blue
               9 skeins dark beige
Tapestry needle
Embroidery frame or stretcher
Burlap
Cotton lining fabric
Sewing needle and basting thread
Hammer and tacks *or* staplegun

METHOD

The chair seat shown measures 18 in
(45 cm) at the front and sides, tapering to
14 in (35 cm) at the back edge. The canvas
is stitched in a repeat pattern of simple
blocks, so you can calculate how many
blocks you should work to fit your own
chair seat.

Stretch the canvas on the embroidery
frame. Baste the outline of the stitching
area on canvas, allowing a margin of 8 in
(20 cm) all around. Mark the center point
of the design with vertical and horizontal
basting threads.

Start stitching at the center of the
canvas, using the charted design as a
guide. Work the areas of medium blue and
light blue in slanting satin stitch first, then
fill in the beige and tan areas using
Leviathan stitch.

FINISHING

When the embroidery is completed,
remove it from the frame and block it.
Allow it to dry thoroughly. Mount the
panel on the chair seat as shown in the
diagrams.

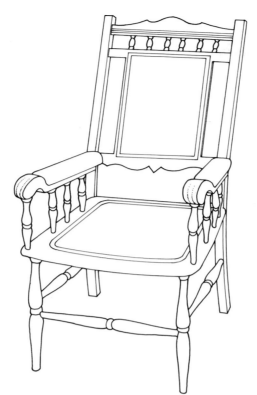

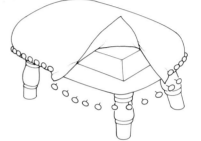

Different types of
wood frame chairs
are suitably
upholstered with
needlepoint. Some
styles have a panel
fitted on seat and
back *(left)*. The
needlepoint is
stretched directly onto
the frame and tacked
in place, with
decorative braid
concealing the raw
edges. Needlepoint
can be used to cover
a small stool *(below)*,
secured at the base
with pins. Pucker the
edges of the canvas
slightly to fit it snugly
around the curved
shape.

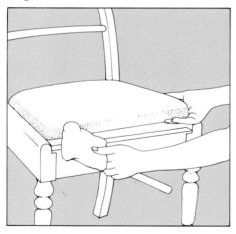

**Replacing the chair
seat** The new
covering on the chair
seat may be difficult
to fit at first. Wrap a
hammer in clean
cloth so you can tap
the seat gently into
place if necessary
without damaging the
needlepoint. Fit the
back edge first and
then ease in the sides
and front.

Right Victorian
embroiderers stitched
panels of Berlin
woolwork for chair
seats and pillows
favoring floral designs
and pictorial motifs.
As in this example,
the flower patterns
were particularly
suited to seat panels
with a curving or
rounded shape.

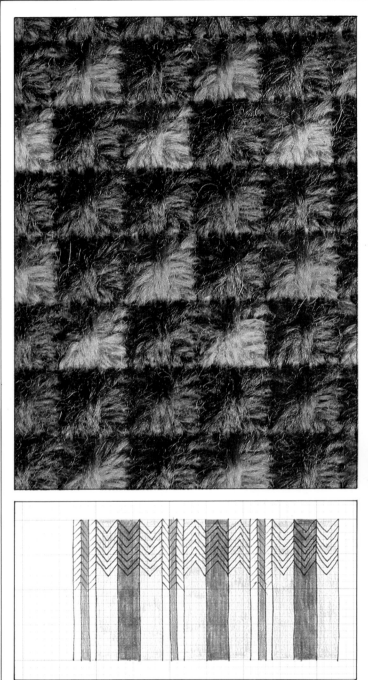

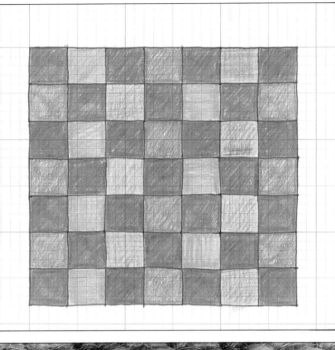

Left This wool embroidery is worked on 10 gauge Penelope canvas. Each square of the chart represents one double Leviathan stitch. The distribution of greens and heavy texture of the stitch combine to give a three-dimensional effect of light and shade. Another color would work just as well, if the same tonal balance were selected.

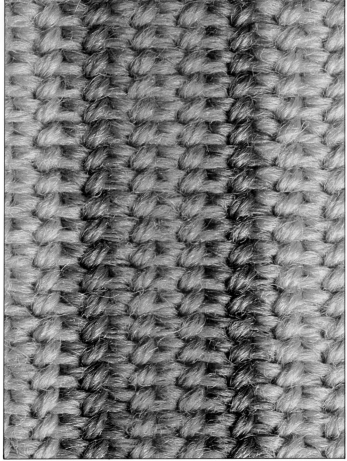

Alternative designs for chair seats

The examples on these pages are all based on simple geometric designs: the variations of scale, color and texture in the stitching create designs of distinctive character, using only blocks and stripes. The squared designs demonstrate two different ways of using a color scheme based on tones of closely related colors, while the trelliswork and stripes are interpreted in subtly muted shades of contrasting colors. Any basic design framework can be elaborated in this way, with reference to the Stitch Directory and the color schemes on pages 38 and 39.

Right Stripes of fern stitch in two shades of grey-green are divided by three lines of tent stitch in cream and deep pink. The tent stitch changes direction on alternate stripes, as can be seen from the color chart *(above)*. The stitching is worked in tapestry yarn on 10 gauge Penelope canvas.

Right Leviathan stitch in pink and purple forms the borders of these blocks, around small squares, each filled with a double Leviathan stitch. The graduation of tones from light to dark in a close range of colors gives a three-dimensional effect and would also be effective worked in cool blue-greens. It is worked in tapestry yarn on 10 gauge Penelope canvas.

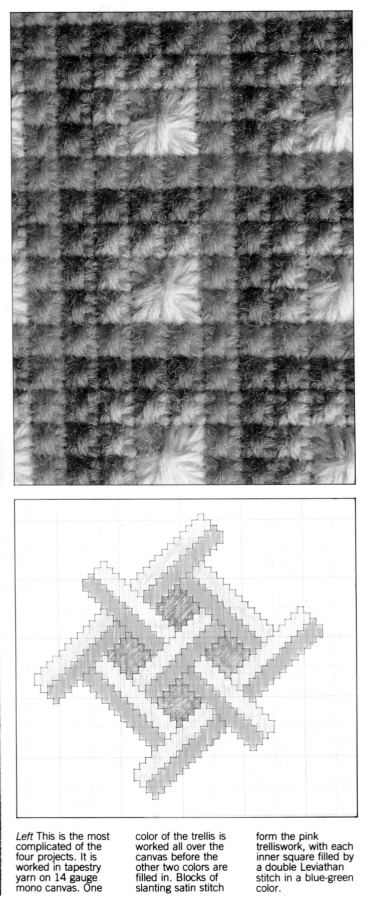

Left This is the most complicated of the four projects. It is worked in tapestry yarn on 14 gauge mono canvas. One color of the trellis is worked all over the canvas before the other two colors are filled in. Blocks of slanting satin stitch form the pink trelliswork, with each inner square filled by a double Leviathan stitch in a blue-green color.

Development of samplers in England

Although samplers were common household objects in the fifteenth century, few pieces have survived from that period. The first written reference to samplers in England is dated 1502, in a document that mentions a length of linen 'for a sampler for the Queen', Elizabeth of York. Twelve samplers were included in a list of Edward VI's possessions drawn up in 1552.

Documentary evidence indicates that the sampler was originally devised and used by adult needlewomen. The embroiderer would keep a record of her favorite patterns and motifs to use as reference or to exchange with a friend. The cloth bearing these stitched designs was called an 'exampler' or 'sampler', terms which derive from the Old French *exemplaire* or *essamplaire*, meaning any kind of pattern that could be copied. A passage from Barnabe Rich's *Of Phylotus and Emilia* (1581) describes how the sampler was used:

> Now when she had dined, then she might go to
> seke out her examplers, and to peruse whiche
> worke would doe beste in a ruffe, whiche in a
> gorget, whiche in a sleeve, whiche in a quaife,
> whiche in a caule, whiche in a handcarcheef;
> what lace would doe beste to edge it, what
> seame, what stitche, what cutte, what garde;
> and to sitte her donne and take it forthe by little
> and little, and thus with her needle to passe the
> after noone with devising of things for her owne
> wearygne.

The earliest surviving English sampler was made by Jane Bostocke in 1598. It is a strip of unbleached linen measuring 17 in (43 cm) by 15 in (38 cm). At the top of the sampler are some floral motifs, a dog carrying its lead, a chained bear, a deer and a heraldic terrier. These motifs, randomly placed on the cloth, are followed by an alphabet and the two inscriptions: 'Jane Bostocke 1598' and 'Alice Lee was borne the 23rd November being Tuesday in the afternoone 1596'. The latter indicates that the sampler was probably intended as a gift for the child. Below the inscriptions a profusion of patterns are stitched haphazardly one after another. The workmanship is of a very high standard and a variety of stitches are included: back, satin, buttonhole, chain, detached buttonhole, ladder, coral, speckling, couching, French knots and two-sided Italian cross. Black beads, seed pearls and metal thread also decorate the work.

Early samplers were stitched at random, but later designs were more formal, with the borders, patterns and motifs carefully arranged in horizontal bands. Some pieces contained as many as 30 different patterns and, because of the sampler's utilitarian nature, designs were shown in the course of construction as well as in completed form. The stitches used were largely dependent on the patterns chosen. Geometric patterns invited the use of satin stitch, which was also popular in whitework. Buttonhole, bullion knot, tent, Gobelin, Holbein, Florentine, Hungarian, Monte-

Above Mary Brewitt completed this band sampler in 1725. It is designed with a religious theme, around the Lord's Prayer situated in the center. The lettering and stylized border motifs are basic cross stitch. The freer-work in the angel motifs is satin stitch with metal thread. Algerian eye stitch is also included.

negrin, cross and Algerian eye are only a few of the many stitches that can be found on these early samplers. Cross stitch was perhaps the most popular of all and was later used so much, particularly during the eighteenth and nineteenth centuries, that it came to be known as 'sampler stitch'.

The design of samplers

Many of the patterns on samplers were taught by one generation to another but, from the sixteenth century on, they might also be copied from sampler pattern books or, more commonly, from books of designs for lace. Italy was the main source of sampler designs and translation of pattern books into English, French and German resulted in a certain ubiquity of motifs. The first printed pattern book was published in Augsburg in 1523 and this effectively put the designs on the open market.

Left Mary Clay put her name to this whitework band sampler in 1696. The name and date have been sewn in colored silk, but the 34 horizontal bands of different styles of alphabet are simple whitework on linen. *Above* This house sampler was worked by Mary Ann Richards in 1800 with colored silks in cross, tent, stem, satin long and short stitches on linen. The inscription rests on two lower corners of heavily embroidered landscape scenes. In this way the sampler combines stylized embroidery with a much freer approach. Parts are unfinished and the original drawing lines show.

107

The earliest surviving pattern book, produced in 1591, is a translation from an Italian work by Vincentio entitled: *New and Singular Patternes for Workes on Linnen and Serving for Patterns to make all sortes of Lace Edgings and Cut Workes; Newly invented for the Profite and Contentement of Ladies and Gentilwomen and others that are desirous of this Art.* Other highly popular books were Shoreleyker's *Scholehouse for the Needle* (1624) and *The Needle's Excellency*, the twelfth edition of which was published in London in 1632. The designs in these books were not all original ideas, but were often copied from patterns on Oriental or Italian silk fabrics. In a period that knew no law of copyright, motifs and whole designs were indiscriminately reproduced from one book to another.

The traditional method of transferring a design from the pattern book to the fabric consisted of outlining the printed design with a series of pinholes and shaking charcoal powder onto the fabric beneath. Unfortunately this practice led to the loss of many old books, as their pages were torn out. Enlargement or reduction of a design was achieved by squaring up or down on a squared grid, much as it is done today.

Many samplers survive from the seventeenth century. During that period the purpose of the sampler changed; it was no longer a source of reference, but an exercise pursued by young girls in the course of their studies. The inclusion of alphabets and numerals suggests that the sampler became increasingly more important as an educational tool. The samplers were usually signed and the age of the embroiderer was often given, together with the date of completion. This evidence indicates that the majority of pieces were worked by girls between the ages of five and fifteen.

Seventeenth-century work generally falls into two categories — 'spot', and 'band' samplers. The 'spot' sampler is one in which motifs are placed haphazardly over the surface, simply to show off the wide range of stitches. The 'band' sampler was usually long and narrow and was sometimes worked from both ends, the designs being carefully arranged in horizontal bands. Whitework, work in colored silks, drawn-thread and cutwork samplers were all very popular. Whatever the purpose of the sampler, the workmanship was usually of a very high standard.

The changing form of samplers

Early samplers were embroidered on linen; the size of the weaving looms controlled the dimensions of the cloth and the samplers might be densely or more sparsely worked with motifs. A highly economical use of fabric was gradually introduced, in which the length of the sampler was dictated by the woven width of the cloth. The selvages of the fabric appeared at top and bottom of the work and the sides were neatly hand-hemmed. The tendency was to work on a long but narrow shape, presumably a few inches trimmed from the end of a full piece of cloth. Many seventeenth-century samplers are only between 6 and 12 in (15 and

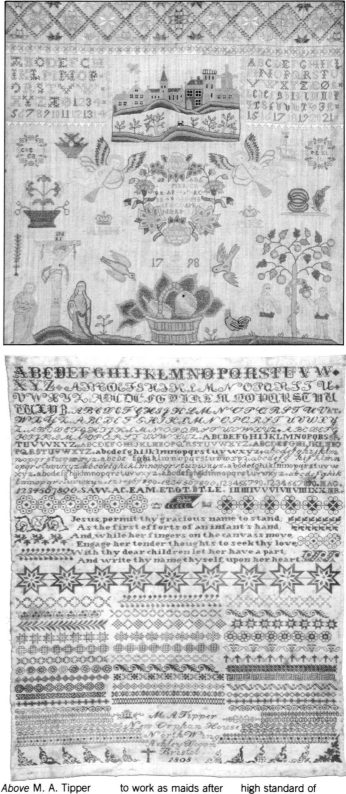

Below Two different alphabets are combined with various motifs to create a well-balanced design in this Danish sampler, completed in 1798 in silk on linen.

Above M. A. Tipper worked this sampler in 1808 at an orphanage in Bristol. Girls would often go to work as maids after leaving an orphanage and there be required to mark the household linen. A high standard of workmanship was expected so the girls would experiment with various designs.

Samplers were originally worked as experimental pieces, to give the embroiderer some idea of the scope of stitched patterns. A number of different stitches would be combined on a narrow strip of fabric, as in this band sampler *(left)*, completed in 1629 and signed by 'Elisabeth'. The motifs — boxers, flowers, acorns — have been worked in Montenegrin, double running and cross stitches. A map of Europe *(far left)* was probably worked by Elisabeth Hawkins, an English schoolgirl, as an exercise in both stitching and geography. Chain and satin stitches are used to show the countries in red and the towns in black. The blue-grey of the sea seems to have been dyed into the fabric.

30 cm) wide, but the length might be two to five times the width. It was the custom to roll the sampler onto an ivory rod so it could be kept to hand in a sewing basket; in this the narrowness of the cloth was an advantage.

The first half of the eighteenth century saw the transition from the long, narrow shape to a shorter, squarer form; the favored fabric was woolen canvas. It is interesting to note that early seventeenth-century samplers are often better preserved than those made even in Victorian times. The linen of early samplers was fairly impervious to damage from moths and damp, but these two factors played havoc with the woolen cloth of later work.

The habit of dividing the sampler into bands continued for a time, together with the use of a few of the old patterns, but gradually most of the seventeenth-century motifs disappeared. Eighteenth-century designs tended to become more naturalistic and were strongly influenced by Indian and Chinese motifs. The sampler took on a pictorial form, combining alphabets and texts with figures and landscape. Samplers were now conceived almost entirely as elementary exercises in embroidery and the practical value of the pattern was negligible. In fact, some of the work shows a limited repertoire of stitches, which suggests that training in needlework had become more perfunctory.

At the beginning of the nineteenth century naturalism left the sampler and was replaced by scattered, stylized motifs embroidered mostly in cross stitch. At this time Berlin woolwork patterns were being imported into England and proved so popular that interest in making samplers declined. (It appears that there was a revival later in the century, when the samplers that were produced were quite innovative.)

Previously, small motifs had remained strictly two-dimensional, but now realistic rendering of complex objects was attempted. This was possible through the use of hand-colored embroidery charts which could be copied on a stitch-by-stitch procedure. Any woman who could work a simple cross stitch could follow a chart to produce quite a sophisticated pictorial representation.

Samplers in Europe

European samplers, while showing various national characteristics, tended to follow the same general line of development as those in England. During the sixteenth and seventeenth centuries, band samplers predominated. In Italy many of these pieces were in cut and drawn thread work, showing the influence of lace designs. This type of decoration was popular for collars, ruffs and personal linen.

German eighteenth-century samplers fell into two distinct types; either small and square with one alphabet surrounded by geometric motifs, or long and narrow with several alphabets and geometric borders, finished with the name of the embroiderer and the date of completion. It was characteristic of German samplers that the stitch selection was far more limited than in English work and from the nineteenth century, cross stitch was the main technique. The colors showed great restraint. Although small mottoes, usually of a religious nature, were to be found, the inclusion of verse never enjoyed the popularity that it did in England.

In the Netherlands, cross stitch also predominated. Eighteenth- and nineteenth-century works were surrounded by the conventional flower border and the motifs were typically Dutch, for example, Delft vases. The quality of stitchcraft in Dutch samplers is not as high as that of some other European countries, but the designs do have charm and it can be seen that they often served as personal records of the life of the embroiderer. Among the later Continental work, Spanish samplers are very distinctive. They were rather large and very decorative, including geometric and floral patterns in brilliant colors and a variety of different threads. Mexican work shows a similar boldness, derived from common roots.

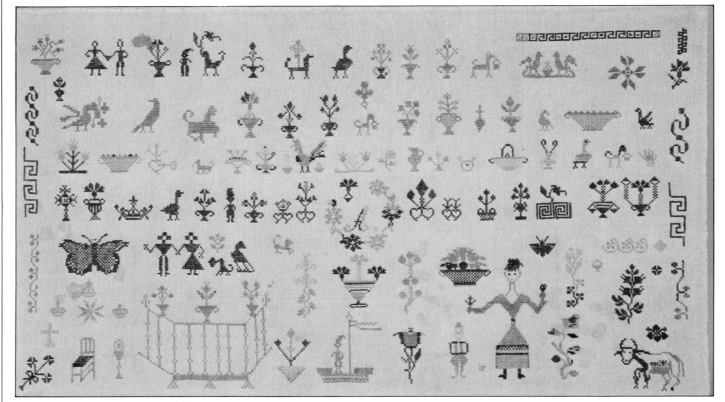

Above This engaging sampler of individual motifs was not signed or dated by the embroiderer, but is thought to be a nineteenth-century piece from Pennsylvania. It is entirely worked in cross-stitch, and although it resembles the randomly worked spot samplers, the design is highly organized and the colors are logically spread throughout the rows of animals, plants, figures and household items.

Right This highly decorative Mexican sampler combines satin, stem, cross and Hungarian point stitches with drawn thread work on linen cloth. Unusually for a sampler of this type, where the main objective was merely to try out stitches, a central pictorial design has been combined with geometric motifs and border sections.

Far right The careful arrangement of a complex design seen in both these samplers is typical of the nineteenth century style of American samplers. The musician with his lute *(top)* was worked in tent, cross and satin stitch on canvas by Rebecca Van Reed Gresemer from Pennsylvania. It includes sections which are hand painted on the fabric. The inscription suggests it was a gift for her aunt. The house sampler stitched by Charlotte Glubb in 1813 *(below)* is a combination of cross and satin stitches, straight stitching and couched work. It is more conventional in design, with the central picture and framing border, but both examples show how inventive American work became during this period.

American samplers

English influence dominated needlework produced during the formative years of the American nation, and was sustained by English teachers going there to work in private schools. The earliest sampler to be found in America is actually English; a cut and drawn whitework example made by Anne Gower in 1610, which she took to her new home on her marriage to Governor John Endicott in 1628. The first truly American sampler that survives is known to have been worked by Loara Standish, completed in 1655. It is identical in style to contemporary English examples, a band sampler without an outer border but with a very intricate design worked on tabby weave linen in two weights of silk. Unfortunately very few seventeenth-century American samplers have survived, but the evidence of those that remain suggests that most stitch and design techniques used in Europe were copied in American work with little adaptation.

In the eighteenth century the population of the American colonies more than tripled in size. Urban growth encouraged a cultured society which demanded artistic refinement. Within this framework, careful attention was paid to the education of young ladies. Thus they were taught creative needlework, the foundation of which was mastery of basic sewing skills by means of a sampler. Some girls went on to finishing schools, where they produced more elaborate and individual pieces of work.

The American sampler began to look like a picture, with one or more border designs acting as a frame around an alphabet, which was set out in rows to demonstrate different designs. Around 1750 the sampler became quite free and naturalistic; elements of the environment appeared, such as landscapes, animals, and people dressed in contemporary costume. A variety of materials contributed to a more realistic style — beads, sequins, metallic threads, human hair, padded silk appliqué and painted paper. It can be difficult to differentiate between pictorial samplers and embroidered pictures from this period. In their book on American samplers, published in 1921, Ethel Stanwood Bolton and Eva Johnston Coe made a somewhat arbitrary ruling by declaring that any embroidery signed and dated by its worker could be considered a sampler.

American samplers were generally worked on rectangular or square pieces of cotton, wool or linen. The stitches, of cotton, silk or woolen threads, included chain, back, eyelet, herringbone, split and stem stitch, French and bullion knots. On the whole there was an inventive use of stitches in work before 1700 but as in England, many samplers of the eighteenth and nineteenth centuries consisted of cross stitch alone. The range of stitches and materials diminished slowly over this time and designs became stylized. A nineteenth-century sampler typically included a verse surrounded by 'spot' motifs, arranged symmetrically on the fabric. Woolen 'tammy', a glazed wool fabric, was popular as a base and, as in European examples on wool, we find that the background cloth has often deteriorated quite badly.

As the machine production of textiles increased it seemed less important to teach young girls embroidery, particularly after the advent of the sewing machine in the middle of the nineteenth century. The great period of the distinctive American sampler ended and in Europe a similar decline occurred. Revival of interest in samplers in our own century has been based on the historical information that they provide and the engaging character of the designs. But the practical value is also being restored and many needlework schools now require a sampler to be made as evidence of proficiency in stitchcraft.

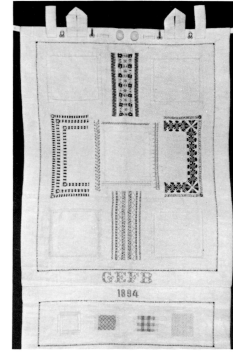

Elements of design

The motifs and designs used in samplers vary considerably and often reflect the country of origin, though many are traditionally shared. In the seventeenth century flower motifs were popular all over Europe. The rose had particular significance in England; first the red rose of Lancaster and the white rose of York, then the two combined in the Tudor rose. In the United States, the widespread appearance of the Tudor rose, strawberries, carnations and tulips is testimony to English influence during the colonial period. Plant motifs are ubiquitous and Averil Colby has identified the symbolic meanings of some of those most commonly used:

Rose — earthly love
Lily — purity or chastity
Honeysuckle — faith
Pear or apple — forbidden fruit
Olive tree — peace and goodwill
Cherry — fruits of Heaven
Pomegranate — hope of eternal life.

Coronets and crowns appeared in embroidery in the eighteenth century, first above initials on household linens and then above initials on samplers. The original function of these motifs may have been to denote noble rank, but it is unlikely that this genuine symbolism would have produced so many. As samplers became increasingly pictorial during the course of the eighteenth century, they featured buildings, landscapes, figures and animals, all portrayed in quite a naturalistic way. These were not randomly scattered spot motifs, but were arranged in balanced compositions and motifs were often matched in pairs.

A curious motif that appeared in the seventeenth century and transmuted gradually over many decades was the boxer, a small figure, originally nude except for a fig leaf, often repeated in rows. The description 'boxer' may have derived from the figure's stance — a stiff pose with arms extended, suggesting an aggressive attitude. Oddly enough, it is possible that the origin of this figure was a popular sixteenth-century design showing a lover with his beloved. Modesty or fashion prompted seventeenth-century embroiderers to clothe the figures and it seems that the female figure gradually disappeared, leaving the man represented by himself. In some designs he is holding out a trophy, which he seems to be offering to a stylized form of a tree. The tree has sufficient signs of human shape to suggest that it may be a corruption of the original female figure.

Decorative borders were introduced into sampler design in the eighteenth century and these included geometric patterns derived from scrolls and Greek fret designs, together with elaborate, interwoven fruit and flowers. In American work, these borders sometimes assumed such importance that they threatened to swamp the central design. The border continued to be an important feature of nineteenth-century samplers where it always enclosed the work on all four sides.

The map sampler originated in schools, combining needlework with geography, which was a subject of increasing public interest in England from around the middle of the eighteenth century. Not until the following century did maps become popular in the United States, and here some surprising misconceptions were revealed. In one map of Europe, the embroiderer shows a common land boundary between England and France.

The variety of subject, motif, pattern and border is endless; as samplers have progressed over the centuries, all of these design elements have been used with increasing ingenuity. More detail about the other common forms in sampler design — alphabets and numerals, mottoes and verses, the family tree, houses and public buildings — are included with the projects in the second part of this chapter, as is the original and often most abstract form, the technical sampler. The embroiderer today has unlimited scope in both design and materials and plenty of encouragement to express individuality, whether traditional motifs and alphabet forms are preferred, or more modern ideas of design are incorporated in the work.

Designing and making your own sampler

Designs for samplers can be taken from many different sources, such as fabrics, oriental carpets, china, lace and Fair Isle knitting patterns. It is also possible to adapt designs from the many exquisite samplers exhibited in museums. When studying existing motifs you may find that you can use part of a composition and omit or rearrange elements of it, with a view to interpreting the original design rather than merely copying it. Reference can also be made to the large variety of embroidery books that are available, some of which present charted cross stitch designs for motifs,

Left Map samplers were first embroidered in the eighteenth century when geography was a popular subject. They were often produced in schools, where they enabled the pupils to practice stitching and to learn their countries at the same time. This map of England completed in 1928 is worked entirely in cross stitch, using different-colored thread to outline the counties and very fine black thread for the town and county names. The color variation for the border lines means that the whole map becomes more comprehensible.

charts you will find that the color of the stitch is indicated either by the color of the square or by a symbol; symbols also designate the sort of stitch to be used. This type of design is eminently suitable for cross stitch but can also be combined with freely worked stitches; in this instance you should work on a close-weave linen using the counted thread method.

Once the basic design has been completed the next thing to consider is the choice of color, which will greatly affect the finished piece. It is advisable to select a neutral color for the background as this will allow the design to be seen quite distinctly. If the background color is too strong it will dominate the finished work and 'drown' the design. Your decisions about color will be made easier if you produce several different colored versions of your original design on paper; bear in mind that slight modifications may have to be made when matching the color of the threads with the color of an inked design.

Colored threads can be applied in different ways depending on the effect you want to create. For instance, when working with natural subjects you can blend and mix the colors in order to recreate their subtle tones in a manner similar to painting. To achieve this result you can either use one strand from each of several colors in your needle at once or use the 'shaded threads' that are commercially available and are particularly suitable for blended areas.

As well as solving design and color problems, you must make decisions about the techniques and materials that can translate the design into embroidery. The threads you choose must be compatible with the weight of your fabric but the design can be enriched by using a selection of different threads, and other materials such as net, beads and sequins. When plain-weave fabrics are used, techniques such as appliqué and fabric painting can be introduced to suggest different textures; examples of this type of work can be seen in some American samplers. Texture and depth can also be created by the careful choice of stitches — flat stitches, such as satin stitch, can be worked on objects to suggest they are in the background, whereas an abundance of French knots forms a textural surface which appears to move to the foreground.

Interesting results are achieved by combining different ways of using both color and texture. Obviously your choice will be dependent upon the theme of your design, the background fabric and your own personal preferences. The possibilities in the selection of designs, materials, colors and textures are endless. There are no rules or set combinations to work from, the final decisions are based upon your own taste and inclination. The sampler was originally a personal piece of reference material and although today samplers are more decorative than educational, they should still reflect your own ingenuity and style.

borders and alphabets. All designs, whatever their origin, will naturally draw your eye either from top to bottom or from side to side and this factor should be taken into consideration.

When adapting a historical design or working to the traditional sampler format, you will need a border pattern, an alphabet and/or numerals and a variety of different motifs which can be placed either at random or asymmetrically in your design; these motifs usually appear in abundance in the lower part of the work. It is important to consider the scale of all these elements, as a degree of consistency is necessary if the overall composition is to appear balanced.

The border pattern can be as simple or as complex as you wish and is usually repeated on all four sides of the work. These border patterns are either abstract or derive from natural subject matter and in some cases they combine elements of both. Pictorial motifs can be derived from virtually any source. Historical examples offer a wide variety of subjects, and the choice of motifs is largely determined by the theme of the work.

Alphabets and numerals are chosen according to the role they are going to play in the work. If they are to be arranged in horizontal rows they can include a variety of capital letters, lower case lettering and numerals usually ranging from 1 to 9, which can be as ornate or as plain as you wish. When letterforms are being considered for a verse or inscription, the design should be fairly simple so that the lettering can be easily read, but it is acceptable to use ornate capital letters in conjunction with simpler lower case ones.

If you are going to work on a fabric that offers a natural grid, even-weave or a patterned plain-weave such as gingham, the designs for all these features can be charted on graph paper. Each square of the graph paper represents one square of the fabric and both are available in several gauges which relate to the number of squares per inch (2.5 cm). In commercially produced

Above This sampler is worked from an embroidery kit and is a modern interpretation of ornamental alphabet design. The letters and animal motifs work closely together so that each animal is fitted to the initial letter of its name. The pictorial element is a method of enlivening this type of sampler and the motifs are represented naturalistically. The whole piece is worked in cross stitch.

ALPHABET SAMPLER

Evidence of domestic needlework over several centuries shows that household linen and items of clothing were customarily marked with the initials or monograms of their owners. In this respect lettering was an early component of stitchcraft and embroidery design. Alphabets and numerals, names and dates were a feature of samplers from the earliest point that the works evolved into more than simple stitch directories. As American and European samplers became products of the schoolroom, the meticulous rows of stitching the equivalent of writing practice in a schoolbook, the inclusion of alphabets, words and inscriptions must undoubtedly have helped children to become familiar with their letters; but the primary function of the sampler remained the development of excellence in needlecraft and the stitching techniques were the main focus of attention.

DESIGNING AN ALPHABET SAMPLER

Many types of embroidery stitches have, at various times, and for various purposes, been adapted to the stitching of alphabets and initials. Lettering in cross stitch has a peculiar charm, owing to the broken contours and angular shapes created by the stitching grid, and it immediately calls to mind the association with many of the finest, most intricate sampler designs. An alphabet is, however, a simple and satisfying vehicle for the beginner in embroidery. Since each character is in itself relatively small and very well-defined, you can quickly progress and gain confidence in the work. It is a useful exercise in color and design, as well as a way of practicing well formed stitches.

THE PROJECT

This sampler has been designed with the inexperienced stitcher in mind. The lettering is bold, the design enlivened by changes of style and scale within each row of letters, to keep the stitcher's interest alive. A very basic but effective cross stitch border frames the alphabet, deliberately kept plain to point up the detail of the lettering. The color scheme exploits the contrast of blue and pink, linked by a mauve related to both colors, but the shades are kept reasonably close so that no one row of characters dominates the design.

The design could easily be altered by the substitution of other alphabet styles and a different border, by reference to the design sections at the back of the book. Study the scale and color relationships carefully so that your own choices are balanced.

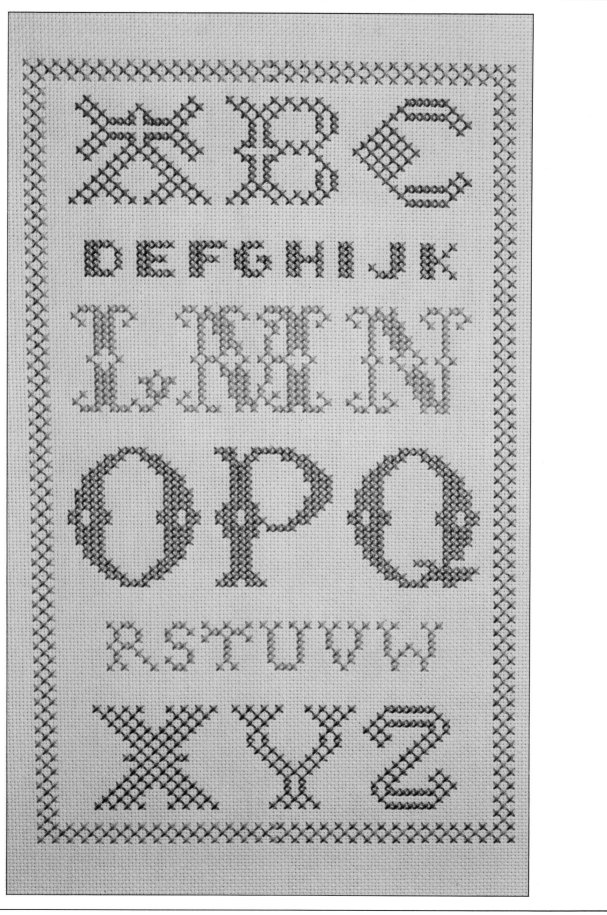

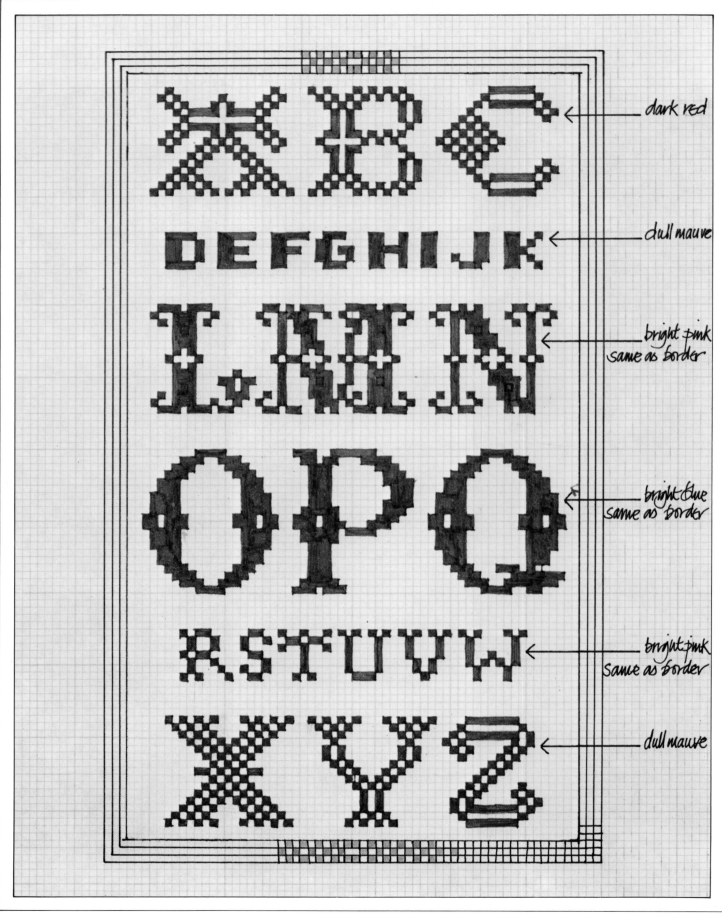

dark red

dull mauve

bright pink
same as border

bright blue
same as border

bright pink
same as border

dull mauve

MATERIALS

Aida even-weave fabric, 18 gauge, in cream
Stranded floss 1 skein of each color
          medium blue
          bright pink
          mauve
          dark red
Crewel needle

METHOD

The finished area of stitching is 12¼ x
7¼ in (31.5 x 19 cm) and you should leave
a 5 in (12.5 cm) margin of fabric on each
side to allow for mounting and framing.

This piece need not be worked in a
frame unless you prefer to do so. If not
using a frame, neaten the edges of the
fabric to prevent them from fraying before
you start the embroidery. The alphabet
and border are worked entirely in cross
stitch, using three strands of embroidery
floss.

Baste the central lines on the fabric and
begin stitching from the center, following
the chart exactly. Each square on the
chart represents four woven blocks in the
fabric.

FINISHING

Press the work lightly on the wrong side.
Mount or frame the sampler as preferred.

These samples show
different types of
lettering that can be
combined in the
design of an alphabet
sampler. Each set
conforms to a grid
that gives a guide to
cross stitching, but
graphic forms from
other sources can
be charted on
graph paper.

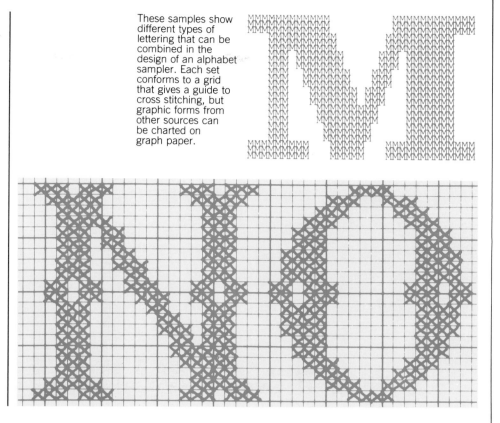

117

MOTTO SAMPLER

Mottoes and verses became a feature of the sampler from the seventeenth century on, and in following centuries such a text was the focal point of the work. These inscriptions, more than any other aspect, provide clues as to the social background of the embroiderer.

Religious and moral verses often appeared, together with the Lord's Prayer and the Ten Commandments. To modern eyes, there is a disconcerting preoccupation with death, even among the youngest needlewomen, presumably a reflection of the poor life expectancy. One verse reads:

> The soul by blackning defiled
> Can never enter Heaven
> Til God and it be reconciled
> And all its sins forgiven.
> Charlotte Roberson. Aged six.
> Time flies. Death approaches.

Inscriptions and records of events were not included in Continental samplers; the only written reference was to the name of the worker and the date of completion. In English work, if a sampler did not include a religious text, it would often bear an inscription referring to children's duties to their parents, or warning the child of the hazards awaiting her later on in life. The dangers of fickle love were recorded on a sampler made by Elizabeth Bock in 1764:

> Oh might God that knows
> how inclinations lead
> Keep mine from straying lest
> my Heart should bleed
>
> Grant that I honour and
> succour my parent dear
> Lest I should offend him who
> can be most severe
>
> I implore o'er me you'd have
> a watchful eye
> That I may share with you
> those blessings on high
>
> And if I should by a young
> youth be tempted
> Grant I his schemes defy and
> all he has invented.

The nature of these verses reflects the fact that the sampler was in all respects an instructional work. One young embroiderer, in 1797, effectively preempted criticism of her needlework or her choice of text by delivering the warning:

> In reading this if any faults you see
> Mend first your own and then find
> fault in me.

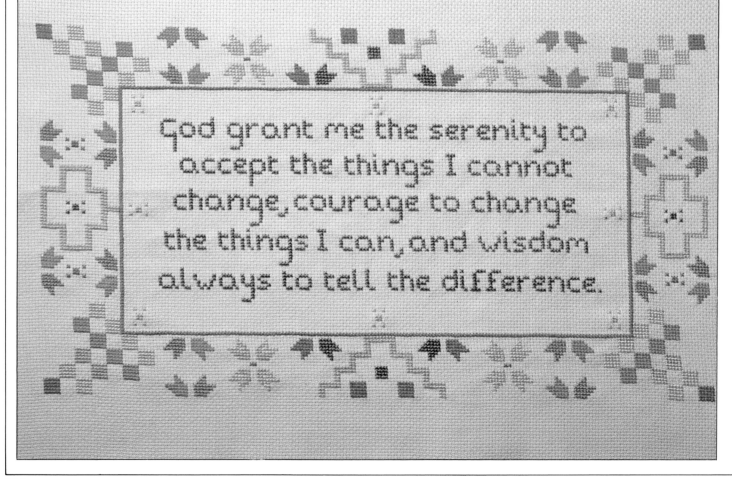

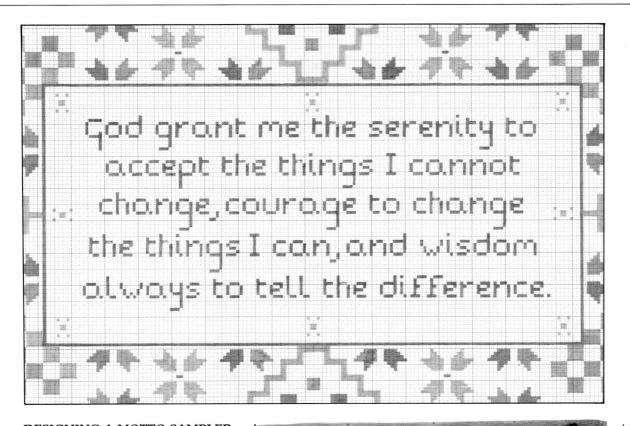

DESIGNING A MOTTO SAMPLER

The moral and religious texts favored in eighteenth- and nineteenth-century samplers had a particular affinity with the style and purpose of the whole work. By studying samplers in museums, you can see how the lettering and motifs have been chosen and combined through a long tradition of sampler embroidery; alternatively, you might want to use a modern proverb or quotation, or a verse from a poem or song, and develop suitable motifs from other sources, such as photographs and contemporary fabric designs.

The lettering should be fairly plain, so the motto or verse can be read easily. Always plan the lettering on graph paper first, to ensure even spacing of individual characters and words. The selection of threads is a matter of personal preference, as long as they are compatible with the fabric.

Color affects the design considerably, and you can change the overall effect of the piece by choosing to work with tones of one color, in closely related colors or with high contrasts. The background can be white, neutral or a definite color; a cool hue, such as grey, pale blue or a light green will enhance the design rather than dominate it. The color can be selected to match the mood of the text — for example, a somber tract could be embroidered in tones of greys, browns and greens, while a verse from a song might be more vivid and lighthearted in the color scheme.

Left This motto sampler was completed by 10-year-old Eliza Richardson in 1837. It is cross stitch worked with colored silks on woolen fabric. The motto has been divided in two by naturalistic motifs, and formalized by a geometric repeat border. The central motifs provide relief from the more regimented surround, and successfully break up the block of writing.

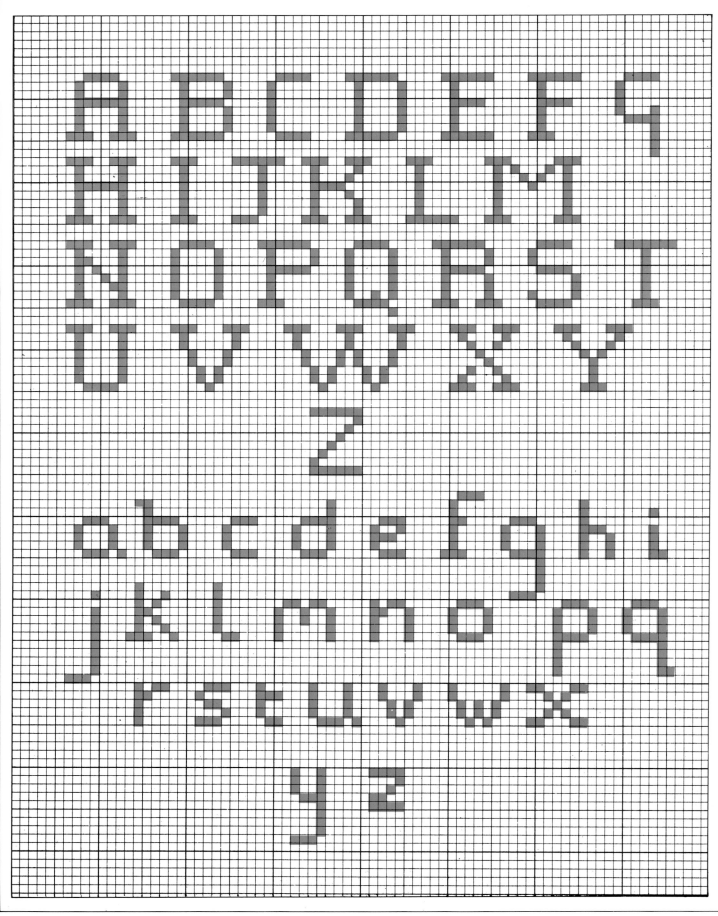

THE PROJECT

The design charted here can be adapted to suit a different motto or inscription. If you want to change the lettering or border pattern, make up a new chart showing the variations. When making alterations to the colors, note the basic range of shades and distribution of harmonies and contrasts.

MATERIALS

Grey binca, 15 gauge
Stranded floss 1 skein of each color
           dark grey
           bright pink
           rose pink
           light emerald green
           pale lilac
           medium purple
Crewel needle

METHOD

Draw up a chart on graph paper, with reference to the working drawing and the motifs given in the diagrams. The piece is worked entirely in cross stitch, using three strands of floss. The stitched area measures 9 x 15 in (23 x 38 cm) and you should allow a 5 in (12.5 cm) margin of fabric all around for mounting or framing.

Mark the center of the fabric with basting stitches. Embroider the lettering first; work from the center outward and follow the chart stitch by stitch.

FINISHING

Check the whole design for missed stitches. Block the work carefully or press it on the wrong side. Mount or frame the sampler as preferred.

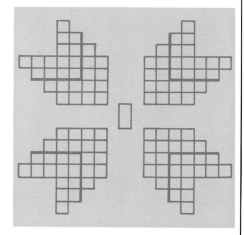

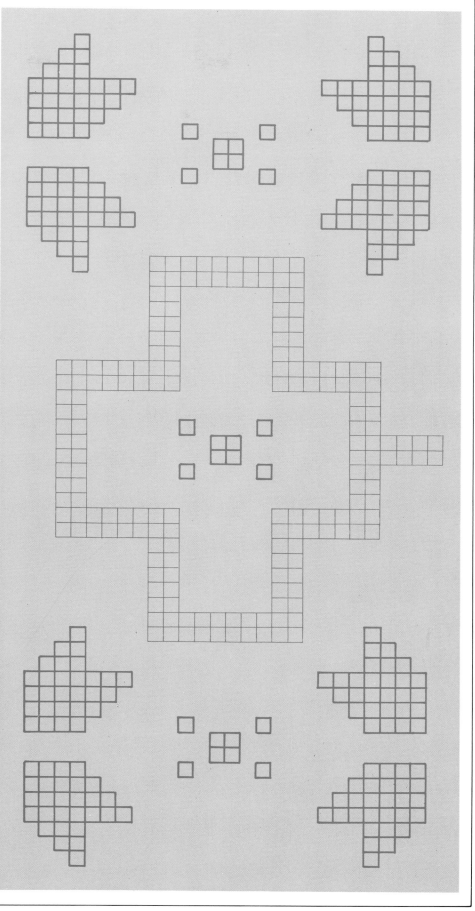

FAMILY TREE SAMPLER

From the early eighteenth century, samplers have been used to record such family occasions as births, marriages and deaths; the popularity of this type of record reached a peak in England and the United States during the nineteenth century. The design and wording of many of the samplers suggests that they were intended as gifts.

Family records produced during that time have a certain poignancy, as they indicate that infant and child mortality were high and life in general rather precarious. In some examples, the names of deceased family members were stitched in black thread. American examples typically record more information than those produced in England, often going back several generations. Spaces left where death dates could be filled in show that the sampler might be considered as work in progress over quite a long period, rather than a record made after the event. Fully worked samplers might deal with a shorter period of time; a sampler from the first half of the nineteenth century records the marriage of Thomas and Elizabeth Markham, and the children subsequently born to them.

Family tree samplers and designs that record marriages and births are still popular today, but many contemporary examples are worked from prepared embroidery kits. It is not difficult, however, having prepared a family tree, to develop and decorate it in the form of an embroidery chart, so you can have a uniquely personal record for your own pleasure or as a gift to a close relative or friend.

Left This is a modern kit for a family tree sampler, designed from an old Danish example. It is entirely worked in cross stitch, combining an alphabet and numbers at the top. The motifs down either side represent the two families, the parents, their crest, and religion. The initials in the center represent the merging of the two sides. The sampler has a distinctive clarity in the color and spacing of the motifs.

DESIGNING A FAMILY TREE SAMPLER

When you design a sampler to show your family tree, the emphasis should be on simplicity in the design, so you can then elaborate it with variations of color and texture in the materials. The lettering should always be kept simple so the names can be easily read, but the border patterns and motifs can be as plain or as ornate as you wish and you could include some more decorative capital letters, provided the initials are clear.

An even-weave fabric is the most suitable background for the design. The regular texture of the weave supplies a grid for both simple cross stitches and more freely worked embroidery, allowing development of texture over the whole area. Any thread can be used that is compatible with the fabric. If the fabric is strong or rather coarse, you can combine woolen yarn with the embroidery cottons to vary the colors and surface effects.

THE PROJECT

This design can be adapted to suit any family tree, by modification to motifs, colors and lettering. In this case the motifs have been chosen to relate to both family backgrounds. You could extract suitable motifs from historical examples or work out designs that have a particular association with a family member. In simple terms, for example, each person can be represented by a geometric or pictorial symbol stitched in their favorite colors.

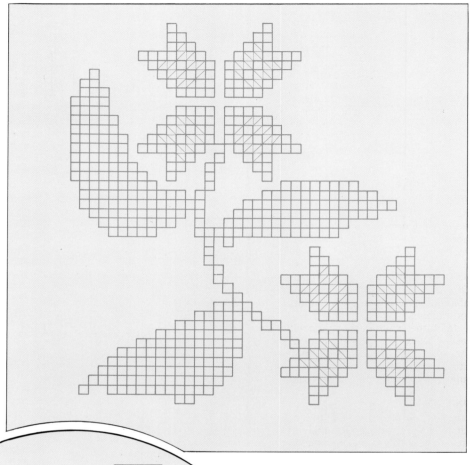

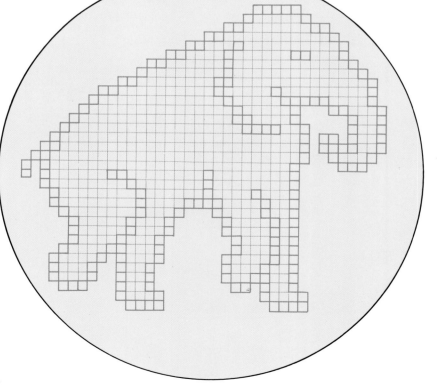

MATERIALS

Aida even-weave fabric, 18 gauge, in pale green
Stranded floss

1 skein of each color

black	light olive green
white	dark jade green
silver grey	yellow green
medium grey	lilac
medium blue	light purple
petrol blue	medium purple
rose pink	dark purple
bright pink	light brown
maroon	medium brown
cream	dark brown

2 skeins of medium green

Crewel needle
Embroidery frame or stretcher

METHOD

Make up a chart on graph paper, using the working drawing and diagrams of motifs as reference. The entire piece is worked in cross stitch, using three strands of floss. The design measures 18 x 12½ in (45 x 31 cm); the grid is 320 squares by 220. Allow a 5 in (12.5 cm) margin of fabric all around to allow for mounting and framing.

Mark the center of the fabric with basting stitches. Mark the center of the charted design and then work on the fabric stitch by stitch, from the center outward, following the charted colors.

FINISHING

Check the finished embroidery for missed stitches. Block the work carefully, preserving the rectangular shape (see page 32) and let it dry completely. Mount or frame the sampler as preferred.

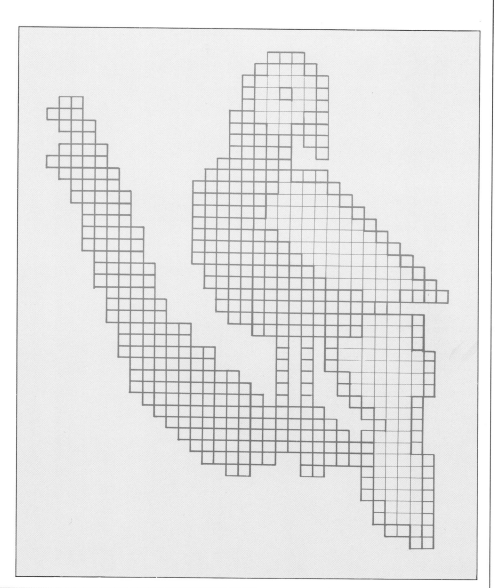

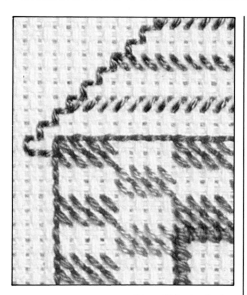

Above This detail of the sampler shows the roof outlined in back stitch and the tiles and bricks indicated with half cross stitch. All other motifs are worked in cross stitch.

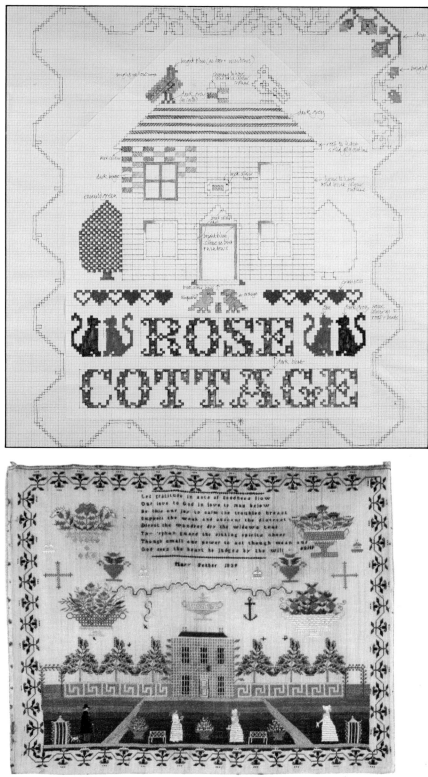

HOUSE SAMPLER

The most popular subject for American samplers in the second half of the eighteenth century was the embroiderer's own home, shown in a two-dimensional, frontal view, or from slightly to one side with a simple indication of perspective. The designs would include members of the family, pets and domestic animals, stylized views of the garden and background landscape, or plant motifs suggesting the surroundings. House samplers have a particular appeal from the point of view of color and design, but in addition they are a fascinating and revealing record of changes in styles of architecture and costume, and can provide unexpected details of the habits of everyday life in town and country.

In England, many Victorian samplers portrayed buildings with great exactitude. A piece worked by Mary Pether in 1839 shows a rather grand house, its grounds, and members of the household. Three women, a man and a dog are all worked in extraordinary detail. There are also pots of flowers, latticed garden seats and a lawn which is naturalistically rendered through grading of the green shades of the thread. Although mansions and large houses were common on nineteenth-century samplers, smaller houses and cottages in country surroundings are also depicted, as well as castles, ruins and archways.

Above Mary Pether's house sampler, dated 1839, is worked in a combination of cross stitch, satin stitch and Algerian eye, worked in colored silks on woolen fabric, with a repeat border on all four sides to frame the piece. The lower half of the work, containing the house, is much more heavily embroidered than the top section with the inscription and flower motifs. The fine detail provides a very good picture of the style of architecture and mode of dress that was fashionable at the time.

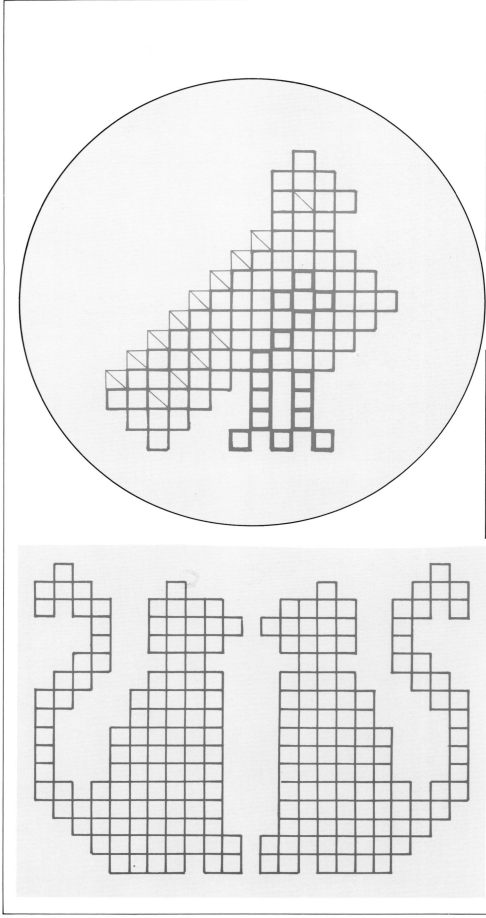

DESIGNING A HOUSE SAMPLER
There are two basic ways you can
approach making a personalized design for
a house sampler, depending on the effort
you are prepared to make in drawing up a
chart. Quite simply, you can opt for a
stylized rendering, choosing suitable
motifs, approximating to your own home
and family, that have already been
adapted for embroidery in cross stitch. A
more ambitious method is to use
photographs of the house, the people who
live in it, the pets and the garden, and
gradually simplify the shapes so they can
be transferred to graph paper. While you
may not be aiming for a naturalistic
impression, it is advisable to use the real
colors as a basis for the embroidery color
scheme. The earthy or neutral tones of
brick, stone and tiling can be contrasted
with touches of bright color in such details
as paintwork, flowers and clothing for the
figures.

Another popular idea in American
sampler design was the representation of a
public building. This could easily be
charted from a photograph or postcard,
with suitable motifs and lettering added,
and would make a pleasing and unusual
memento of a local landmark or well-
known monument.

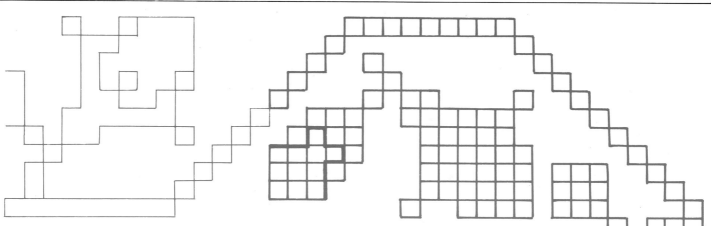

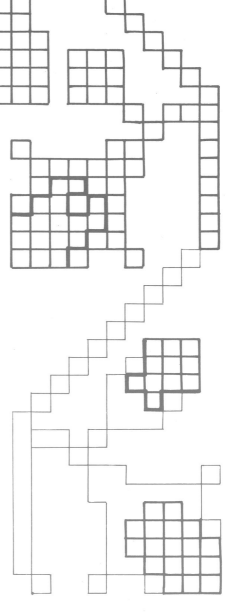

THE PROJECT

This sampler has been designed from an actual building called 'Rose Cottage'. The name is reflected in the twining rose border around the outside and a further personal touch is the motif showing the two cats who live in the cottage. The basic framework of the design could easily be adapted to show your own house or apartment, with the motifs changed to suit your taste. Choose from the selection of motifs, borders and alphabets at the back of the book or develop your own ideas based on photographs or drawings. Make sure the lettering you select is easy to read and in keeping both with the style of the house itself and with other details of your design.

MATERIALS

Aida even-weave fabric, 18 gauge, in cream
Stranded floss

    1 skein of each color

bright pink	bright yellow
bright blue	orange
royal blue	brick red
turquoise	crimson
bright green	ginger
dark green	deep beige
dark grey	

Crewel needle
Embroidery frame or stretcher

METHOD

Draw a chart on graph paper, using the working drawing and diagrams of the motifs as reference. The finished area of stitching is 9½ x 7½ in (24.5 x 19.5 cm) and you will need a margin of 5 in (12.5 cm) of fabric all around to allow for mounting and framing.

This piece need not be worked in an embroidery frame, but a better result will be achieved if one is used; there is a great deal of stitching involved and you may find it difficult to keep the work in shape if the fabric is not held taut.

Baste the central lines. The majority of the design is worked in cross stitch; the exceptions are the house wall and the roof, which are first outlined in back stitch, and a few details that are added to the shapes using half cross stitch. Two strands of floss are used for the stitching throughout.

FINISHING

When the stitching is finished, press the work lightly on the wrong side. Mount or frame the sampler, as preferred.

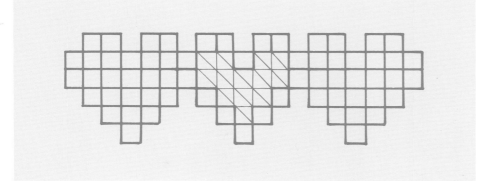

STITCH SAMPLER

The original purpose of the sampler, to act as a stitch directory and pattern reference, was revived during the eighteenth and nineteenth centuries when pieces were worked by professional needlewomen as guides for amateurs. The range of these samplers is highly impressive.

The American sampler tradition of working a variety of stitches within a pictorial framework is another way of showing off fine needlecraft. Many examples demonstrate quite complex illustrative effects, as well as a high standard of skill in stitching.

DESIGNING A STITCH SAMPLER

For a complex pictorial effect, you will need to plan the design and stitching quite carefully so that motifs, patterns and shapes fit together simply and well. You will then be able to experiment with color and texture, including the use of different materials — a variety of threads, beads, sequins and even small sections of appliquéd fabric, for example. The choice of materials and stitches can be as restrained or ambitious as you like, but there must be a basic compatibility between threads and fabric.

THE PROJECT

This design updates the pictorial sampler tradition and the subject matter and stitching techniques have been carefully matched. It demonstrates the use of beadwork and fabric painting combined with embroidery; the stitches are flat and satin stitch, cross stitch, back stitch, closed herringbone and French knots. The background fabric is a close-weave canvas that makes a particularly good ground for fabric painting. Plain and shaded embroidery threads are used to vary the color effects.

MATERIALS

Close-weave canvas
Stranded floss
    1 skein of each color
    light blue   light pink
    royal blue   cerise pink
    lilac   purple
    light, medium and dark green
    3 close tones of silver grey
    shaded threads light pink
                  dark pink
                  green
Crewel needles
Embroidery frame or stretcher
Fabric paints in grey, pale blue and pink
Soft paintbrush
Marker pen
Glass beads in pink and green

Right A particularly fine English example of a stitch sampler, produced in the early nineteenth century, consists of long, narrow strips of fabric bound with ribbon and sewn together. As well as a variety of stitches and designs, this piece demonstrates a mixture of different materials, including silver thread, beads, wool and silk on a linen ground; cross, Hungarian, satin, Florentine and brick stitches are combined with laid and couched work.

METHOD

Stretch the canvas on the frame so that it is fairly taut. Square up the printed design (*below right*) and mark out the shapes on the canvas with a marker pen. Use a pen with non-waterproof ink so that any mistakes can be easily washed out. The design area measures 8 x 10 in (20 x 25 cm) and you should have a 5 in (12.5 cm) margin of fabric all round to allow for mounting and framing.

With the fabric paints, paint the background area grey, the window panes pale blue and the squares of the tablecloth pink. Allow the paints to dry and fix them, if necessary, according to the manufacturer's instructions.

The window frame, teapot, vase and flowers are worked in satin stitch. The leaves are a combination of flat and satin stitch and the flower stems are embroidered in back stitch. Work each area using three strands of floss. The shaded threads automatically create the color variations in the teapot, vase and flowers whereas the tulip leaves and window frame are shaded with separate tones laid side by side.

When working the decorative borders along the bottom, mark the canvas with small squares to facilitate even distribution of the cross stitch, closed herringbone and French knots.

The beads are sewn on last, by either of the methods shown in the diagrams, in a regular pattern repeating four rows — one row in plain pink and one in plain green alternated with rows of both colors combined.

FINISHING

When the sampler is complete, remove it from the stretcher. If traces of the marker pen are still visible you can remove them by washing the whole sampler gently in warm, soapy water. If the sampler is washed, block it while it dries to keep it in shape. Mount or frame the sampler, as you prefer.

Key to the stitch sampler design

Painted canvas
A Pale blue
B Pale grey
C Red and white

Stitch code
1 Satin stitch
2 Satin stitch
3 Satin stitch
4 Satin stitch
5 Cross stitch
6 Closed herringbone
 stitch and French
 knots
7 Flat stitch
8 Satin stitch
9 Beadwork

Bead couching

Sewing beads individually

Motifs

Motifs for cross stitch embroidery can be taken from a wide variety of sources. The long tradition of cross stitch throughout the world has created a vast collection of motifs and patterns designed specifically for stitching, but designs of personal interest or significance — a monogram, a repeat motif for a border or a symbolic device — can be taken from pictures, photographs and printed texts and transferred to a chart for cross stitching. The designs in this section demonstrate how this transition is achieved, and further modifications can be made, such as enlarging or reducing the motif, by reference to the techniques shown on pages 29 and 30.

Borders and corners

Borders are used to create a frame for a rectangular shape, such as a tablecloth, pillow or sampler, and as an edging device for a strip of fabric or the hem of a garment. They are a valuable feature of design for all sorts of embroidered items, as the border can be made narrow or deep, according to the dimensions of the object and other motifs in the design, and you can also use the border to elaborate a simple framework or create a neat, unobtrusive edging for more complex pictorial work.

There are various different ways of creating a border pattern. A narrow border might be two or three rows of cross stitch in different colors, to form stripes or an alternating checkered effect. There are many designs incorporating simple geometric motifs repeated along the strip; a one-way design can be turned at the center

of the border strip, to enliven a basic pattern. Pictorial motifs can be used to construct a border, repeated in rows or matched in pairs with one motif reversed. More complicated designs include twining borders, in which the length of each section is altered to fit different patterns and motifs together, or heavy composite borders, effectively used in Greek peasant work, where bands of patterns and motifs are stitched one above the other to create a deep border with many variations in the design.

There are different ways of treating the colors of a border. It can be stitched in a single color on a solid background of even-weave fabric, or in several different colors on a single-toned background, which can be left plain or filled with stitching. On a patterned fabric, the colors can be designed to disrupt the pattern, as in the gingham skirt border shown on page 80, and another interesting effect is the device of stitching the

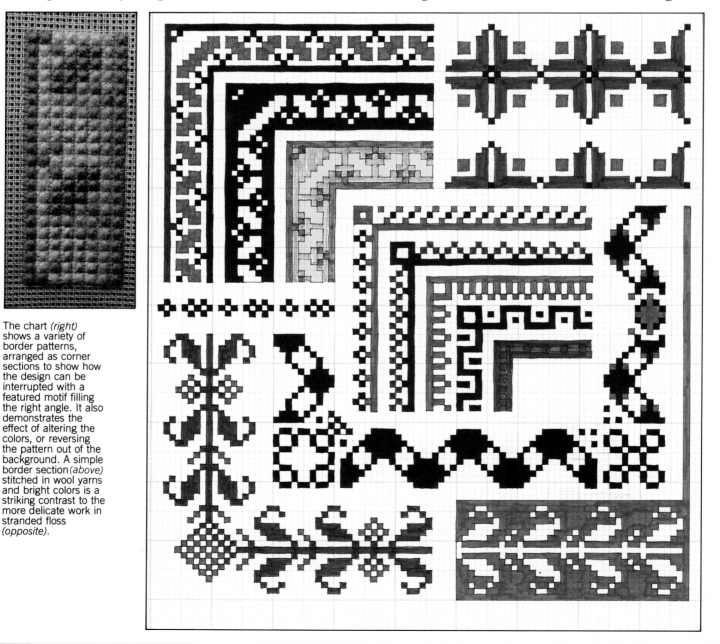

The chart *(right)* shows a variety of border patterns, arranged as corner sections to show how the design can be interrupted with a featured motif filling the right angle. It also demonstrates the effect of altering the colors, or reversing the pattern out of the background. A simple border section *(above)* stitched in wool yarns and bright colors is a striking contrast to the more delicate work in stranded floss *(opposite)*.

background only, leaving the motifs to show as bare fabric. As in Assisi embroidery, unstitched motifs may be outlined with double running stitch to give sharper definition.

Scale and texture are important aspects of embroidery design that can be used to vary the qualities of border patterns. The size of the border should be in keeping with the scale of the whole item; if used as a frame it should not overwhelm the central section of the design and can be kept quite simple, but if it forms the main body of the design, in a skirt hem or table runner, for example, it can be as complicated and colorful as you like. The scale can be altered in the stitching, by using a naturally larger stitch or working a simple stitch across four blocks of the fabric weave instead of only one. The texture can be varied by offsetting flat areas of cross stitch with more elaborate raised stitches. The textural qualities will also be different according to the texture of the base fabric — a fine common-weave, light or heavy even-weave, fine or coarse canvas.

When border patterns are used to frame a design, there is the problem of what to do with the corners, where one section of the border runs into another. This is usually solved in one of two ways: by using a mirror to reverse the border and turn the design at a 45° angle, or by filling the corner with a block of pattern or a single motif that breaks the sequence of the strip border. If a corner block is used that stands out from the basic pattern, it can be made a special feature or integrated with the rest of the design by careful use of the same colors.

A long, continuous border is often more interesting if it is split up into sections. You can run the sections along the length with a small gap in between, or insert a motif to break up the continuity.

This is a stitched sample of the border sections shown in the top left corner of the chart on the facing page. It is worked in stranded floss on even-weave fabric. The slightly openwork effect of the cross stitches creates textual interest. Each strip shows exactly the same pattern worked in different colors: *(from left to right)* the pattern stitched in two colors the pattern in silhouette on a black background; the border completely filled with stitching; the same colors as the previous sample, but with the background to the design left plain.

All these borders are based on simple motifs repeated side by side. In the geometric and heart borders *(right)*, the motifs are alternately one way up and then the other, and each has been designed in such a way that this arrangement has a rhythmic continuity. A stylized pictorial motif of a cat *(below)* is repeated in pairs, with one motif reversed in each pair, and in a straight row, with all the cats facing in the same direction.

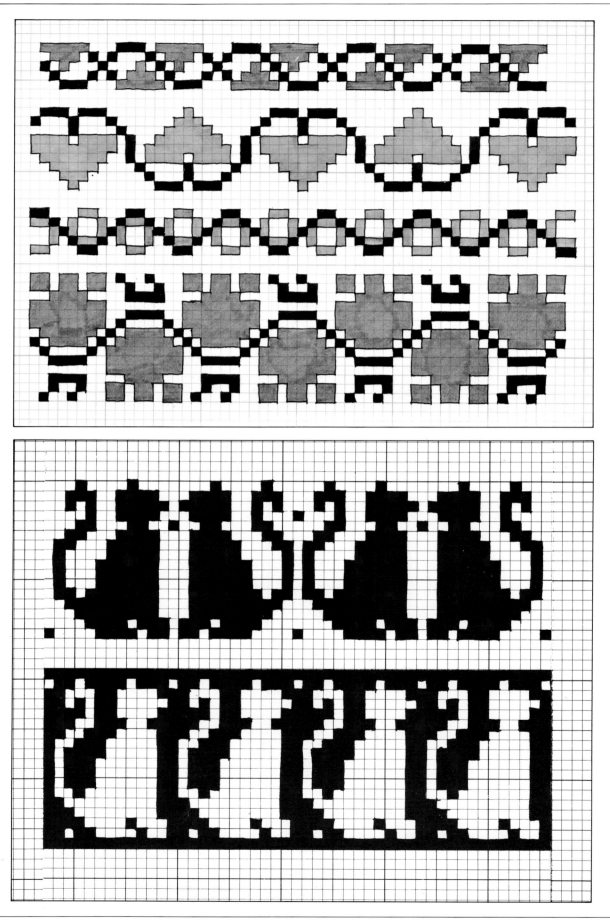

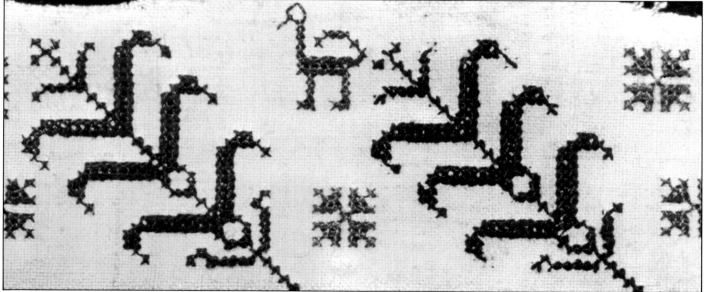

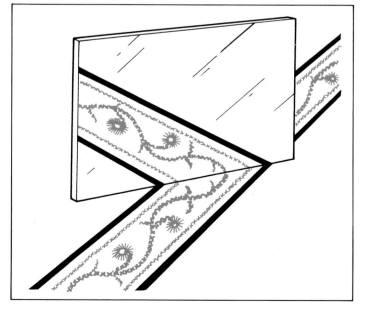

Using a mirror to design corners (left)
The neatest way to turn a border, without inserting a right-angled motif to fill the corner, is to set a small mirror bisecting the corner at 45° and use the reverse image to chart the intersection and the continuation of the design. The pattern is reversed at each corner.

Top A border section worked in Italy in the seventeenth century is stitched in red silk on linen fabric. It consists of a repeat pattern of two stylized floral motifs linked with elaborate linear designs. *Above* Simplicity can be a striking quality, as shown in this Greek border pattern of the eighteenth century.

Monograms

Letterforms worked in cross stitch have been a traditional feature of embroidery for centuries, notably as a practical form of identification in initials stitched on household linen. They are also familiar from the neat rows of alphabets that were so often part of the stitching exercises carried out in samplers. Frequently, initial letters were overlapped, locked or intertwined to form a monogram. Today, monograms are favored more as decorative devices for clothing and can be used to personalize accessories or gift items, such as a fabric bag or belt, handkerchiefs or table linen. A stitched monogram is also an attractive and unusual decoration for a greeting card. If the fabric edges are finished neatly the embroidery can be glued to the card, or framed in a window mount.

Simple monograms are easily designed from any alphabet adapted to a grid form that serves as a stitching guide. Letterforms included in the Projects, or in the Pattern Directory at the back of the book, will provide a starting point for your own design. You can quickly try out different ways of combining the initials in a single device by tracing them off one after the other and allowing the second initial to overlap or interlock with the first, adding a third or fourth if required. When you arrive at a pleasing design, copy it out on graph paper and chart the colors.

An effective monogram must be legible and of a suitable size for the particular item to be decorated. A small, well-defined motif is ideal for a shirt pocket, for example, but to fill the back of a jacket, you need a design that is not only much larger, but also more complex. You can elaborate the device with different colors and textures of thread, or by using more complicated stitches to vary the surface qualities in each section of the design. If you are working on a handkerchief, sheet, or similar item in which both sides may be visible, you might prefer to use the cross stitch variation known as double-sided cross stitch, because the embroidery forms a neat row of crosses on both sides of the fabric.

If you want to make a monogram from letterforms which are not already adapted for cross stitch, you will have to make up a chart on graph paper, modifying the shape of the letterforms as necessary to fit the grid. As shown here, even curved and curling letters can be adapted for cross stitch, but the more exaggerated the form, the more difficult it may be to achieve satisfactory outlines on a squared chart. You can also decorate the lettering with tiny abstract or floral motifs, or add a narrow border to underline or surround the monogram, to make a simple design seem more detailed.

It is easy to work the embroidery on canvas or even-weave fabric, but if the monogram is applied to clothing, the pattern or weave of the fabric may not be sufficiently regular to provide a stitching grid. You can then baste a piece of canvas in place and work the stitching through both the canvas and the base fabric. When it is complete, cut the surplus canvas close to the stitching and use a pair of tweezers to pull out the canvas threads that remain beneath the stitches.

This monogram is stitched on a common-weave fabric with irregular warp and weft. To work the stitching evenly, the device is charted on graph paper *(below left)*, and then a piece of closely woven canvas is tacked over the common-weave *(below)* to provide a corresponding grid for the stitches. The canvas is afterward trimmed close to the stitches and the remaining threads are pulled out from underneath.

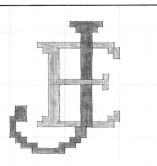
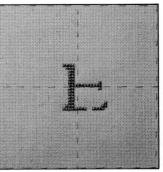

One of the simplest ways to form a well-balanced monogram is to align the vertical strokes of two letters *(below)*. This example, stitched on even-weave fabric, is given a decorative garland and the color scheme is a pairing of opposites.

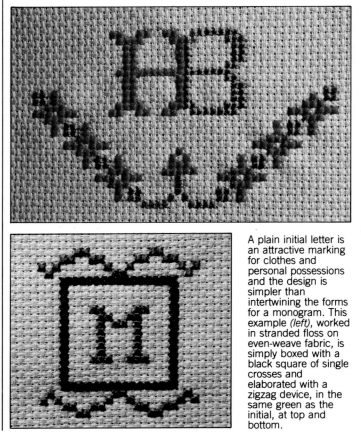

A plain initial letter is an attractive marking for clothes and personal possessions and the design is simpler than intertwining the forms for a monogram. This example *(left)*, worked in stranded floss on even-weave fabric, is simply boxed with a black square of single crosses and elaborated with a zigzag device, in the same green as the initial, at top and bottom.

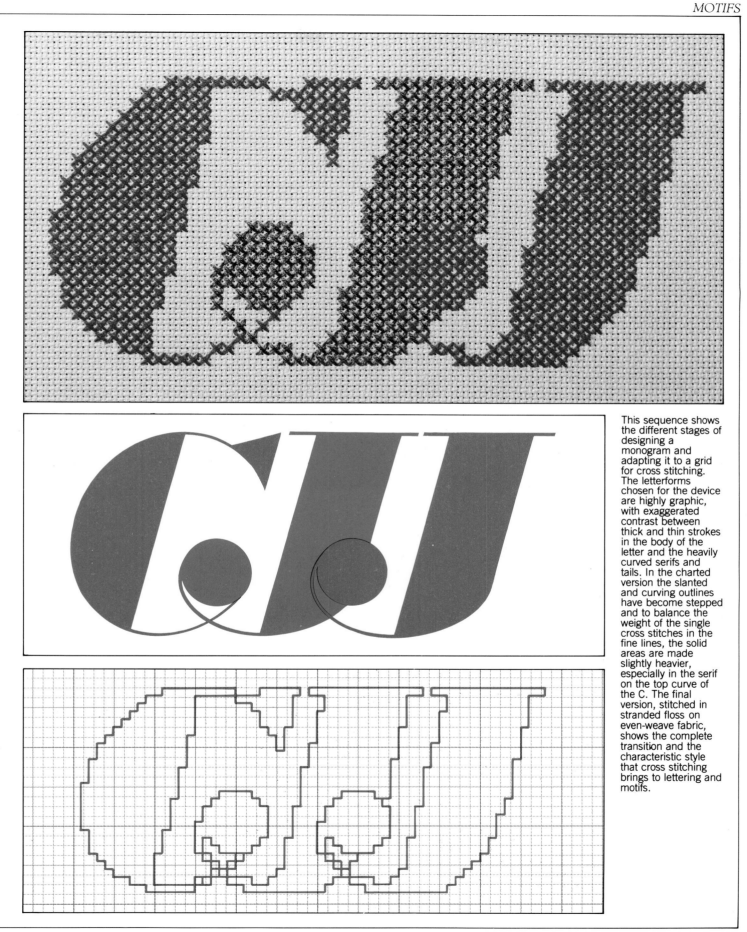

This sequence shows the different stages of designing a monogram and adapting it to a grid for cross stitching. The letterforms chosen for the device are highly graphic, with exaggerated contrast between thick and thin strokes in the body of the letter and the heavily curved serifs and tails. In the charted version the slanted and curving outlines have become stepped and to balance the weight of the single cross stitches in the fine lines, the solid areas are made slightly heavier, especially in the serif on the top curve of the C. The final version, stitched in stranded floss on even-weave fabric, shows the complete transition and the characteristic style that cross stitching brings to lettering and motifs.

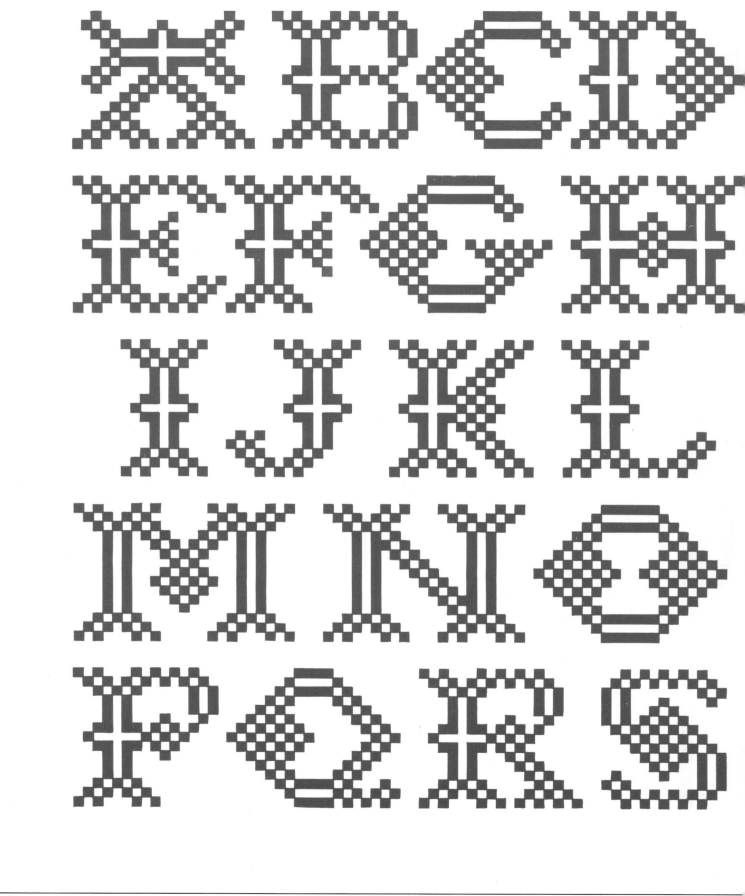

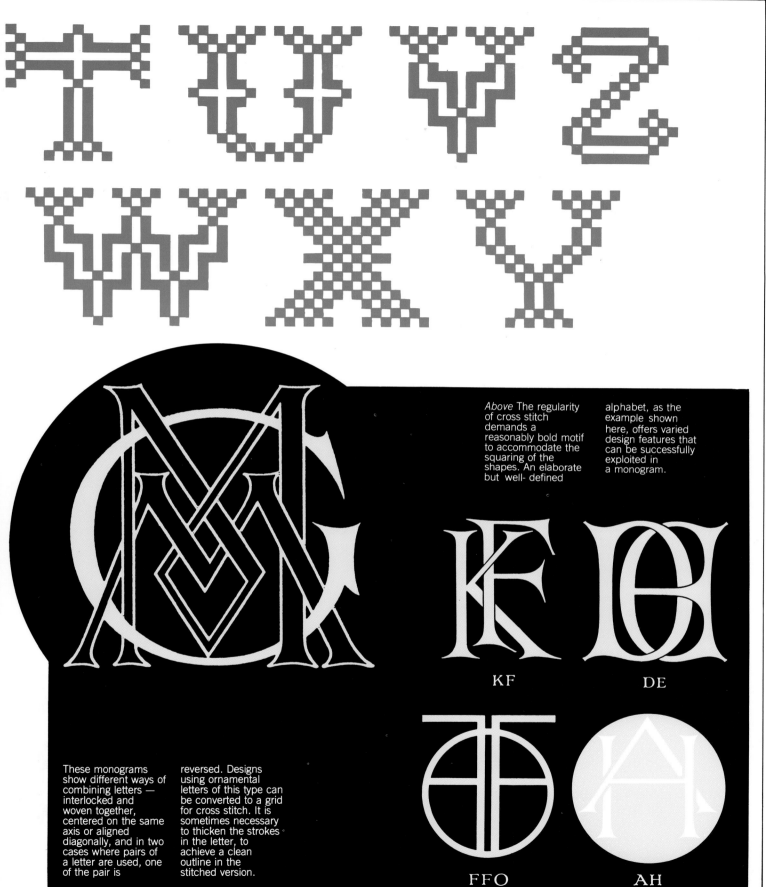

Above The regularity of cross stitch demands a reasonably bold motif to accommodate the squaring of the shapes. An elaborate but well-defined alphabet, as the example shown here, offers varied design features that can be successfully exploited in a monogram.

KF

DE

These monograms show different ways of combining letters — interlocked and woven together, centered on the same axis or aligned diagonally, and in two cases where pairs of a letter are used, one of the pair is reversed. Designs using ornamental letters of this type can be converted to a grid for cross stitch. It is sometimes necessary to thicken the strokes in the letter, to achieve a clean outline in the stitched version.

FFO

AH

Heraldic symbols

Heraldry developed in Europe primarily as a functional rather than a decorative art. Heraldic devices were used to establish ownership, through the use of carved seals, and identity in tournaments and on the field of battle, by the wearing of a coat of arms. The coat of arms was passed from one generation to another and signified historical continuity, a heritage more important than the individual bearer. At the present time, this symbolism is still fulfilled in heraldic devices belonging to royalty and aristocracy, and many corporate bodies — commercial and government institutions — possess heraldic insignia which are a mark of identity and stability of tradition. Symbols derived from heraldry are also used in the emblems of schools, colleges, universities and formal societies.

While the granting of a hereditary coat of arms requires official sanction, heraldic imagery is an interesting source of motifs for less formal designs. The lion and unicorn, a crown, coronet or crest, a national emblem, and the basic element of the shield which bears the coat of arms, are all items that can be interpreted as motifs for embroidery and there are a number of stylized plant and animal forms. In essence the symbols stand for continuity, therefore heraldic design has been traditional rather than innovative. The devices and colors were originally bold and stylized, to serve as immediate identification.

As heraldic design has been elaborated over centuries, a distinctive feature is the curvilinear style, with flowing contours and intricate decoration. Much of the detail can be abandoned in design for cross stitch, as a fussy motif is ineffective unless worked on an unusually large scale, but the most important modification is the translation of curving shapes to the angular grid of a chart for cross stitching. The design is inevitably simplified and made more geometric, but careful choice of threads and stitches will give the motif a decorative character of its own.

Stranded floss and pearl cotton are the most appropriate threads, as they have a natural sheen that enriches the design. A more flamboyant touch can be added with metallic threads; these can be stitched separately or combined with strands of floss, depending upon the effect you require. The background fabric should be either canvas, if you intend to stitch the whole surface, or a suitable even-weave fabric providing a neutral or colored base for the motifs. The stitching should be kept small and even, so closely woven fabric is a better choice than a coarse mesh, but you can develop the textural qualities of the design by varying the stitches, for example, combining tent stitch with basic cross stitch and its simpler variations.

Heraldic symbols were occasionally used in sampler design, as individual spot motifs or repeated to form intricate borders. The devices shown on these pages demonstrate the principle of adapting the shapes from a drawing or photograph to the graph paper grid, and this can be applied to any formal device or decorative emblem that could be used as an alternate motif for your own projects.

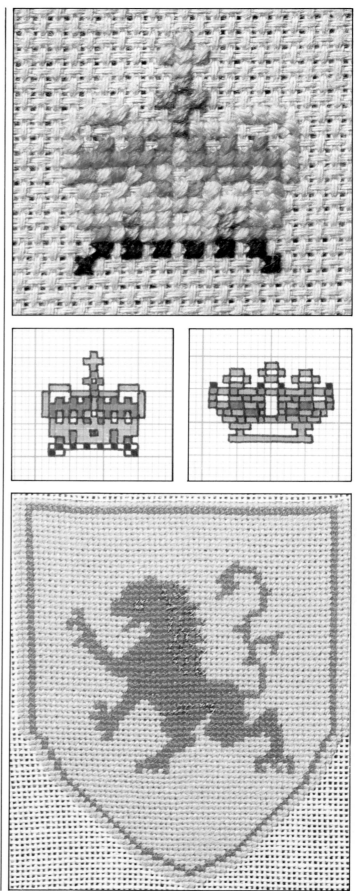

Three different
heraldic devices are
here adapted to cross
stitch. The crown *(far
left above)* is worked
on colored even-
weave fabric, so the
background needs no
stitching, while the
shield with the
heraldic lion *(far left)*
is fully stitched in
stranded floss and
metallic thread. The
curving shape of a
unicorn *(above)* is first
charted on graph
paper to angularize
the shapes and then
stitched on a close-
weave canvas. The
bold outline sharpens
the effect and adds
elegant definition.

143

Alphabets and Motifs

*These pages contain alphabets, border patterns and motifs designed on
a regular grid. They can be worked directly in cross stitch on an even-
weave fabric or canvas by the method of counting threads, or you can
copy them on graph paper to make up a chart as a stitching guide to
your own design.*

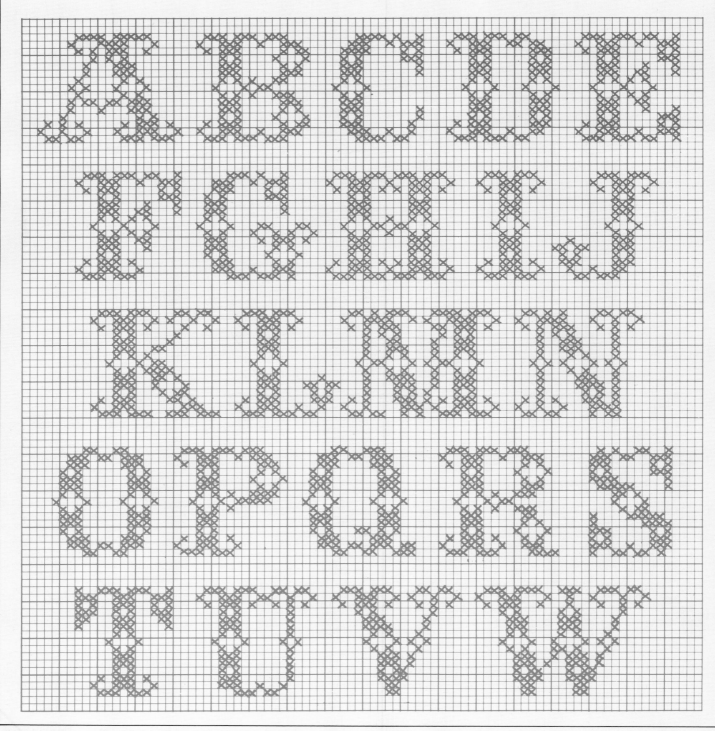

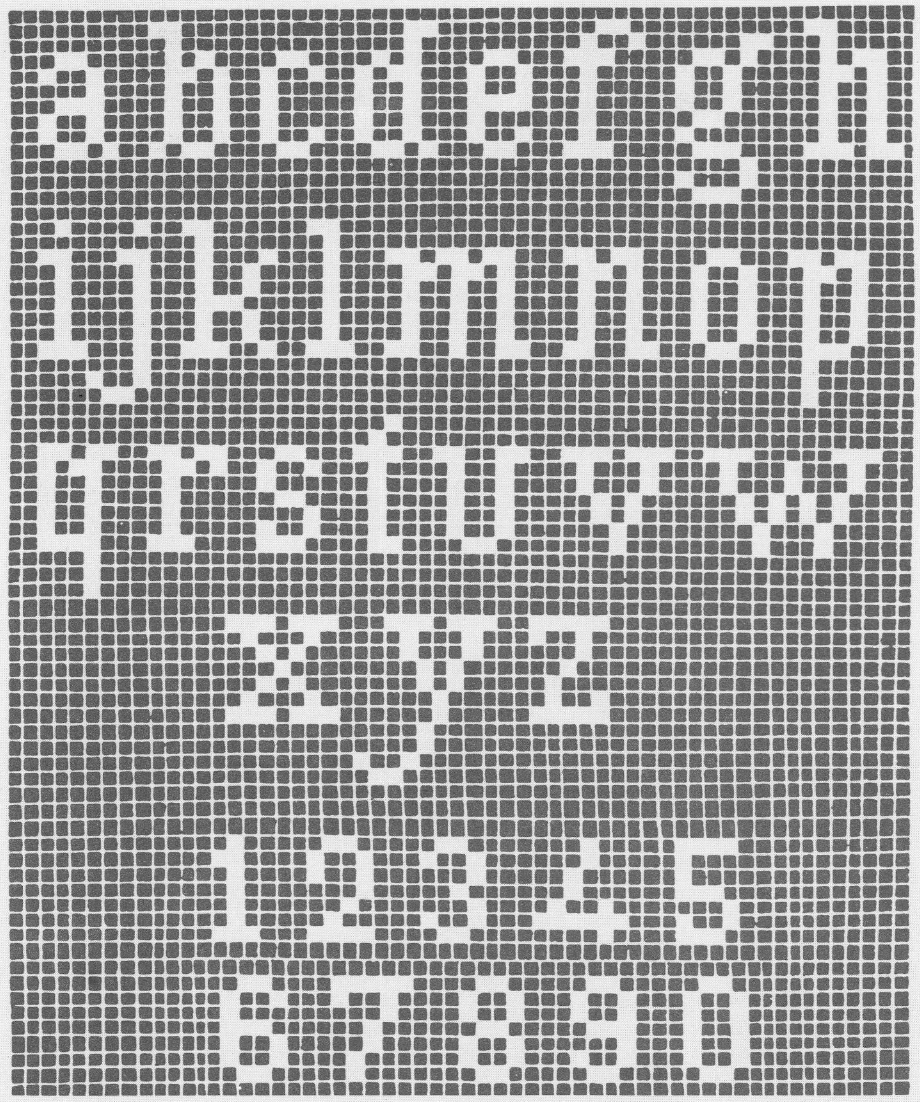

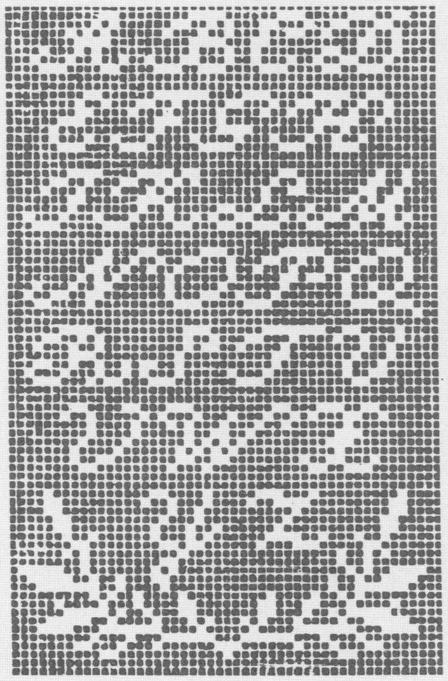

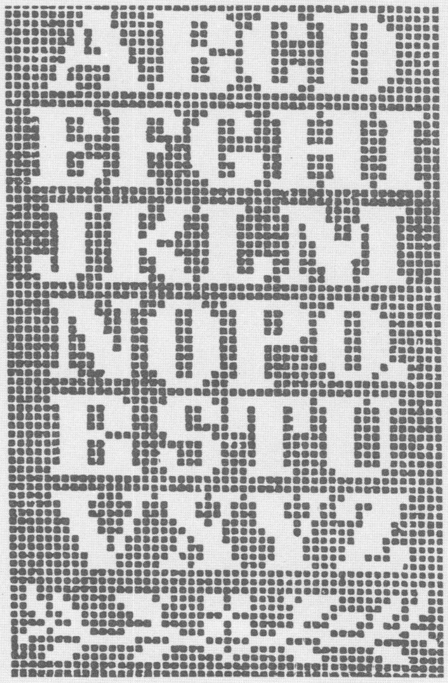

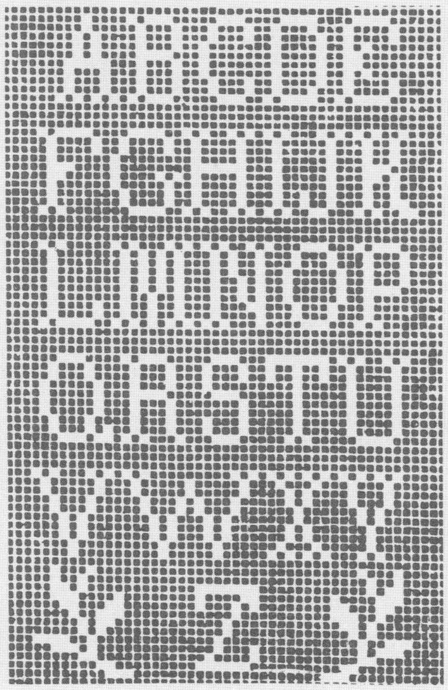

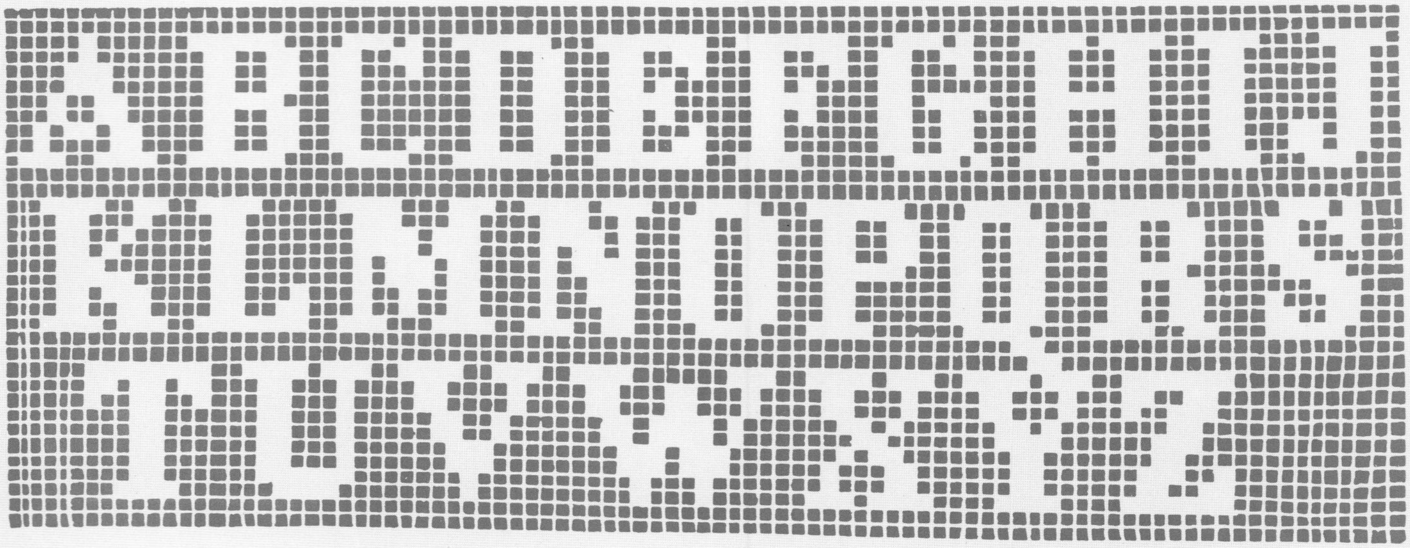

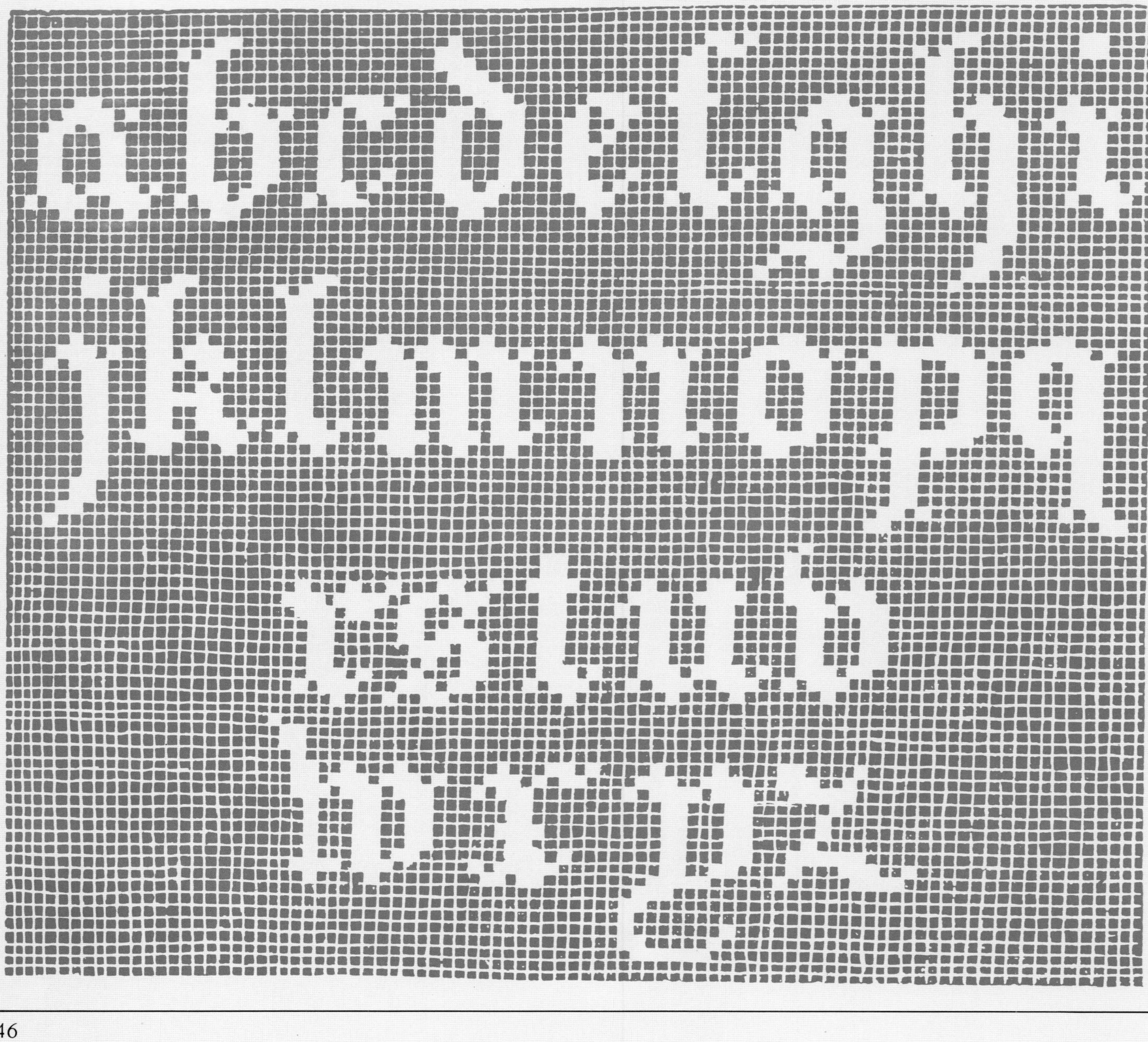

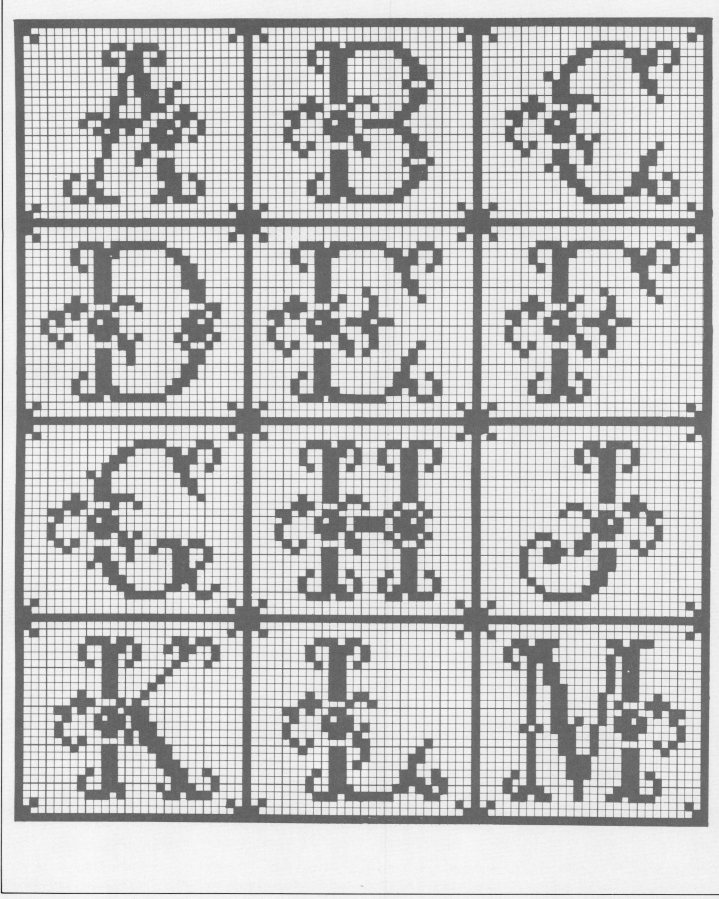

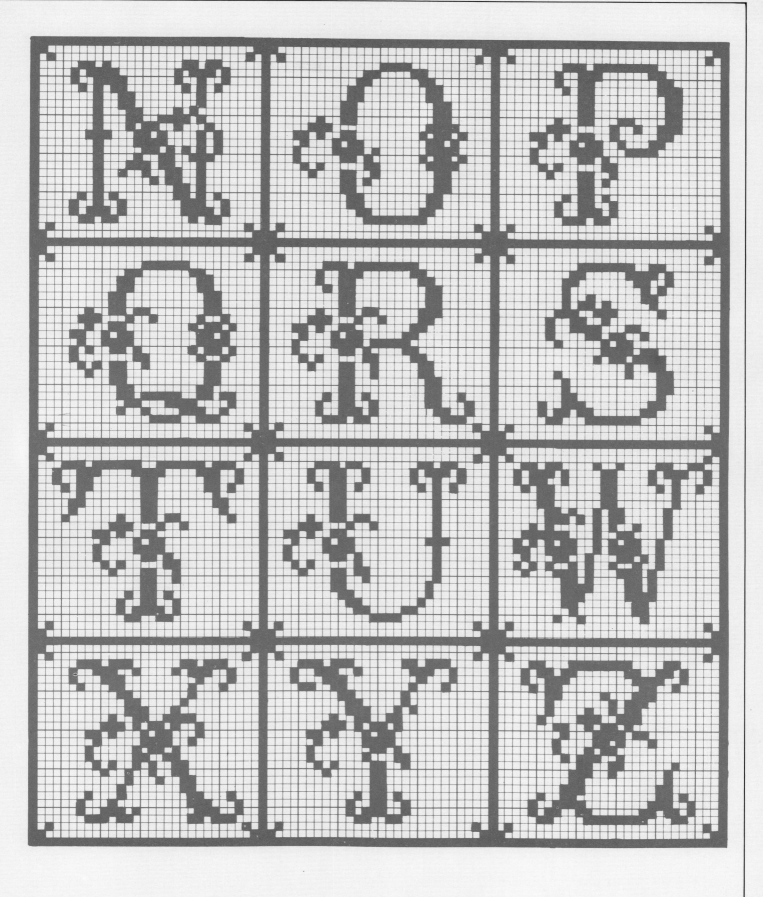

Glossary

American crewelwork Eighteenth-century CREWELWORK in America developed characteristics distinct from similar work in Europe. Due to a scarcity of threads, designs were worked more sparsely; the background was often left unstitched and the MOTIFS became specifically American — for example, describing indigenous fruit and flowers.

Applied work An embroidery technique in which one fabric is placed on another and sewn down with either decorative stitches or small invisible ones. The technique has been traditionally used in making heraldic banners. It is often combined with patchwork and is very popular today in the making of decorative panels.

Assisi work A technique of COUNTED THREAD WORK in which patterns or MOTIFS are left unstitched while the background is filled with plain or long armed cross stitch.

Band sampler A SAMPLER with a typically long and narrow shape. The designs were carefully arranged in horizontal bands and the stitching was sometimes worked from both ends.

Bead couching A method of stitching beads to fabric by threading the beads and COUCHING the thread to the fabric with a small stitch between each bead.

Beadwork A decorative technique particularly popular in the seventeenth and eighteenth centuries, when beads were applied to fabric either to make a complete design or to highlight a stitched MOTIF.

Berlin woolwork A technique of working designs in colored yarn on canvas, following a chart in which the design is shown in grid form, each square representing one stitch. The yarns and charts were originally produced in Germany, but the method became very popular throughout Europe and the United States in the nineteenth century.

Blackwork or chicken-scratched This technique, used on clothing and household linen, was most popular in the sixteenth century. It consists of outline and filling stitches worked in black thread on linen, to create geometric designs, often including MOTIFS of flowers and fruit.

Blocking The process of smoothing and squaring a finished piece of embroidery by dampening it with water and pinning it into shape on a flat surface, where it is left until thoroughly dry.

Boxer A MOTIF popular in seventeenth-century embroidery, originally showing a small figure nude except for a fig leaf. Clothed figures also gradually became common. The description 'Boxer' may have derived from the figure's stiff pose, suggesting an aggressive attitude.

Canvas A ground material for embroidery in which vertical and horizontal threads are woven together to produce precisely spaced holes between the threads. The fabric has a regular grid-like structure and is available in different weights and thicknesses.

Canvaswork See NEEDLEPOINT.

Chenille needle A long, thick needle with a sharp point and a large eye.

Common-weave fabric A fabric in which the WARP and WEFT threads are not woven regularly enough to provide a grid for embroidery by COUNTED THREAD techniques.

Complementary colors Pairs of opposite colors, consisting of one PRIMARY COLOR and the SECONDARY COLOR formed by mixing the other two primaries. The complementary pairs are red/green, blue/orange, yellow/purple. The pairings have a mutually enhancing effect.

Cording A strip of bias-cut fabric folded lengthways to enclose a thin cord. It is inserted into a plain seam to give a decorative finish.

Coton à broder A tightly twisted, pearlized thread. It is similar to PEARL COTTON, but with a less lustrous finish.

Couching A method of tying down one or more threads laid on a GROUND FABRIC, by stitching over them at regular intervals with another thread, to form an outline or solid area of stitching. It is particularly suitable for textured and metallic threads that are not easily drawn through the fabric.

Counted thread work A term that refers to several different embroidery techniques, the common factor being that the scale and placing of the stitches is determined by counting the WARP and WEFT threads of the GROUND FABRIC over which each stitch is worked.

Crewel needle A needle of medium length and thickness, with a sharp point and a large eye.

Crewel yarn A fine 2-ply yarn for delicate NEEDLEPOINT or free embroidery.

Crewelwork Embroidery stitched with CREWEL YARNS on a linen background, using a variety of stitches to create freely worked designs. In traditional crewelwork the MOTIFS were often represented naturalistically and were usually plants and animals rather than geometric designs.

Cutwork A technique in which MOTIFS or patterns are outlined with close buttonhole stitching and the GROUND FABRIC is cut away in various sections of the design.

Darned net A pattern formed in the squares of net fabric with closely worked darning stitches. This type of work has been popular all over Europe from the Middle Ages to the present day, originally using hand-made net and later machine-made fabrics.

Double canvas See PENELOPE CANVAS.

Drawn thread work A type of embroidery in which threads are drawn from the GROUND FABRIC and the spaces left are then filled or edged with different stitches. There are many forms of this technique, including HARDANGER EMBROIDERY and NEEDLE WEAVING.

Even-weave fabric A fabric with WARP and WEFT threads that are identical in thickness and provide the same number of threads over a given area, enabling stitches to be worked by counting the threads.

Fabric painting A method of coloring COMMON-WEAVE FABRIC with specially prepared dyes, paints or crayons, all of which must be fixed to make the color permanent. The fabric is stretched on a frame while it is painted.

Gauge The number of threads which can be stitched in an inch (2.5 cm) of CANVAS. Also the number of threads or woven blocks which can be stitched in an inch of EVEN-WEAVE FABRIC

Gold embroidery Stitching with threads made of gilt, or gold strands wound around silk, used in a variety of embroidery techniques including COUCHING. The technique was most widely used during the Middle Ages and Renaissance, particularly for ecclesiastical garments.

Graph paper Paper printed with a grid of equidistant vertical and horizontal lines.

Greek fret pattern A geometric pattern from ancient Greece which was introduced into all kinds of ornament in the late eighteenth and early nineteenth centuries. The fret pattern was often used as a decorative border in SAMPLERS.

Ground fabric Any fabric on which embroidery is worked. See CANVAS, EVEN-WEAVE FABRIC, COMMON-WEAVE FABRIC.

Hardanger embroidery A DRAWN THREAD technique that originated in Norway and was used particularly on household items. It is worked on open-weave, double-thread linen with thick linen or cotton threads.

Hoop A round frame for stretching the GROUND FABRIC while the embroidery stitches are worked.

Interlock mono canvas CANVAS with a 'locked' construction, formed by vertical threads made up of two thin threads twisted around each other, and round a single, thicker, horizontal thread. It is more stable than MONO CANVAS.

Matte embroidery cotton A tightly twisted 5-ply thread, fairly thick and with a matte finish, used as a single thread.

Mono canvas CANVAS in which the weave is formed by the intersection of single vertical and horizontal threads. It is also known as single canvas.

Motif Part of a design that can be isolated as a single unit. Often geometric or stylized in form, it may be featured singly, or repeated to form a border or allover pattern.

Needlepoint A general term for embroidery worked on CANVAS. Typically, the entire surface of the canvas is covered with stitching and a wide range of stitches can be used. Needlepoint is also known as canvaswork.

Needle weaving A form of DRAWN THREAD WORK popular in Eastern Europe and Scandinavia, in which colored threads are darned or woven into a pattern to take the place of threads that have been removed from the GROUND FABRIC.

Pattern book A book of designs printed especially for the use of embroiderers or lacemakers.

Pearl cotton A twisted 2-ply thread with a lustrous sheen. It cannot be divided into separate strands, but is available in three different thicknesses.

Penelope canvas CANVAS in which the weave is formed by the intersection of pairs of vertical and horizontal threads. It is also known as double canvas.

Persian yarn A loosely twisted three-strand wool which can be divided into separate strands.

Pictorial sampler A SAMPLER in which the stitches are worked into a pictorial image, rather than as rows of patterns or single MOTIFS.

Pouncing A method of transferring a design to fabric. A series of pinholes are made outlining a design drawn up on paper, then a fine powder (pounce) such as charcoal is shaken through the pinholes onto the fabric beneath.

Primary colors Red, blue and yellow: in color theory, the purest colors of the spectrum, which cannot be mixed from any others.

Pulled fabric work A technique in which stitches are pulled tight so that the threads of the GROUND FABRIC are bound together and the design is created both by the stitching and by the holes in between.

Raised work Any type of embroidery that is made three-dimensional by the use of some form of padding — for example, cardboard, felt, cotton or wool.

Reticella An early form of CUTWORK which consisted of withdrawing threads from the fabric and working patterns in buttonhole stitch over the remaining threads.

Sampler A piece of embroidery originally worked by an adult needlewoman as a directory of stitches, patterns and MOTIFS, used as technical reference. Samplers later became needlework exercises carried out by schoolchildren for practice in different stitching techniques.

Scroll frame A rectangular embroidery frame on which the GROUND FABRIC is stretched while the embroidery is worked. It is adjustable for different lengths of fabric.

Secondary colors Orange, green and purple; each is formed by a mixture of two PRIMARY COLORS, respectively red and yellow, blue and yellow, blue and red.

Seed pearl A tiny pearl used as extra decoration in embroidery. Each pearl is drilled with a small hole so it can be stitched down on fabric.

Single canvas See MONO CANVAS.

Spot sampler A SAMPLER exhibiting MOTIFS placed haphazardly over the fabric, simply to show off a wide range of stitches and techniques.

Stranded floss A loosely twisted, slightly shiny six-strand thread. For fine embroidery, the threads can be separated and used singly or in twos and threes.

Stretcher A wood frame of fixed proportions on which a GROUND FABRIC is stretched while the embroidery is worked. It can also be used as the framework for mounting a finished embroidery.

Tabby-weave The most common form of all fabric weaves, it consists of WARP and WEFT threads woven alternately under and over each other in a regular sequence.

Tapestry needle A long, thick needle with a blunt tip and a large eye.

Tapestry yarn A tightly twisted 4-ply woolen yarn used in NEEDLEPOINT.

Valance A hanging strip of embroidery attached to a bed, canopy or the top of a window frame. It was usually gathered or pleated and often embellished with tassels or braid.

Warp The threads in a woven fabric that run lengthwise on the weaving loom.

Weft The threads running across the width of a woven fabric, that are interwoven with the WARP threads.

Whitework A term referring to all types of embroidery which may be worked in white threads on white fabric. They include CUTWORK, DRAWN THREAD WORK, PULLED FABRIC WORK.

Index

A

Aida fabric, 22
alphabets:
    calligraphy, *13*
    examples, *144-49*
      monograms, 138; *138-41, 153*
    samplers, 108, 113, 114-17; *12, 108, 114-17*
alternate cross stitch, 45; *42, 45*
American embroidery, 10, 11
American samplers, 110, 112, 127, 128, 130; *12, 110-11*
appliqué, 94; *94*
Arabs, 9
Assisi embroidery, *12*
Azemmour embroidery, *14*

B

Babylonia, 8
baby's bib, 76
back stitch, 64; *63; 64*
backgrounds, color, 37, 38
badges, 95, 142; *95*
    bird motif, 95; *95*
    geometric, 95; *95*
band samplers, *9, 106, 107*
basket stitch, 44; *42, 44*
basting, transferring designs, 27; *27*
beads, 9, 10, 11
bedlinen, borders, 92; *92*
belts, border pattern, 91; *91*
Berlin woolwork, 11, 17, 109; *16*
biblical texts, 118-19
bibs, 76
Binca fabric, 22
bird motifs, *14*
blocking, 31-2; *31, 32*
blouse, with net appliqué, 94; *94*
Bock, Elizabeth, 118
bonnets, *19*
borders:
    bedlinen, 92; *92*
    belts, 91; *91*
    corners, 134-5; *134-7, 151*
    decorative gingham, 80; *80-1*
    gingham tablecloths, 97; *96-7*
    lampshades, 90; *90*
    motifs, 134-5; *134-7, 150-2*
    peasant embroidery, 18
    photographic frames, 93; *93*
    samplers, 112
Bostocke, Jane, 106
boxer motifs, 112
Brewitt, Mary, *106*

C

calligraphy, *13*
    see also letterforms
canvas, 10, 11, 22-3
    blocking, 32; *32*
    mitering corners, *91*
    stitches for, 67
    transferring designs, 28; *28*
caps, 38
carbon paper, 27; *27*
Centennial Exposition, 17
Central America, 8
chair seats,
    needlepoint, 98-103; *98-103*
charting designs, 31
chenille needles, 23
China:
    cross stitch in, 18; *15*
    origins of embroidery in, 8, 9
cholas, 11, 14
Church vestments, 9; *10*
Clay, Mary, *107*
closed herringbone stitch, 53; *51, 53*
Colby, Averil, 112
color:
    borders, 134
    charts, 39
    designing with, 37-8; *38-9*
    Indian designs, *15, 38*
    peasant embroidery, 18
    samplers, 113
    texture and, 39
common-weave fabrics, 22
    stitches for, 67
Copts, 8
cording, 73
corners:
    design using a mirror, *137*
    mitering, *89, 91*
    motifs, 134-5; *134-7, 151*
coton à broder, 23
cotton fabric, early, 8
counted thread work, 8, 9
Crete, 8
crewel needles, 23
crewel yarn, 23
cross stitch, 44, 107; *42; 44, 45*
    alternate, 45; *42, 45*
    crossed corners, 61; *61*
    development of, 9-11
    diagonal, 45; *42, 45*
    double, 45; *45, 46*
    double sided, 48; *46, 48*
    earliest known, 8
    European tradition, 9, 10
    long armed, 48; *46; 47, 48*
    oblong, 48; *46, 48-9*
    oblong with back stitch, 49; *46, 49*
    origins, 8
    St George, 49; *46, 49*
crossed corners cross stitch, 61; *61*
Crusaders, 9
cutwork samplers, 108

D

Danish samplers, *108, 123*
design:
    charting, 31
    color, 37-8; *38-9*
    dimensions, 31
    enlarging, 29; *29*
    heraldic symbols, 142; *142-3*
    motifs, 133-53
    reducing, 29; *30*
    samplers, 107-8, 112-13
    scale, 135
    sources, 10, 11, 107-8
    texture, 135
    transferring, 27-9, 108; *27, 28*
development of cross stitch, 9-11
diagonal cross stitch, 45; *42, 45*
dimensions, calculating, 31
display, 3
djillayeb, 15
dot stitch, 65; *65*
double back stitch, 53; *53*
double cross stitch, 45; *45, 46*
double herringbone stitch, 56; *51, 56*
double Leviathan stitch, 60; *58, 60*
double running stitch, 65; *9, 65*
double sided cross stitch, 48; *46, 48*
drawn-thread samplers, 108
dyes, 8; *38*

E

Eaton, Governor Theophilus, 11
Edward VI, King of England, 106
Egypt, Ancient, 8, 9
'Elisabeth', *109*
Elizabeth I, Queen of England, 10
Elizabeth of York, 106
embroidery:
    origins of, 8-9
    peasant, 18, *15, 18*
Endicott, John, 111
England:
    contemporary embroidery, *12*
    cross stitch in, 17; *8, 10, 13, 17, 62, 66*
    samplers in, 106-9; *9, 59, 106-9, 112, 113*
equipment:
    frames, 23
    miscellaneous, 23
    needles, 23
ermine stitch, 52; *50, 52*
even-weave fabrics, 22
    stitches for, 67
evening shirt, 77

F

fabrics, 22
    Aida, 22
    Binca, 22
    blocking, 31-2; *31. 32*
    canvas, 22-3
    common-weave, 22
    early, 8, 10
    even-weave, 22
    Hardanger, 22
    linen, 8, 22
    linsey-woolsey, 11
    mitering corners, *89, 91*
    preparing, 24
    samplers, 108-9. 111
    transferring designs, 27-9; *27, 28*
family tree samplers, 123-5; *122-5*
fern stitch, 52; *50, 52*
firescreens, *66*
fishbone stitch, 52; *50, 52*
flat stitch, 52; *50, 52-3*
flax, 8
flowers, *see* plant motifs
Ford, Nabby, *12*
frames, 23
    rectangular, 26; *26*
    rotating, 26; *26*
    round, 25; *25*
    scroll, 26; *26*
    using, 25-6
framing, 33, 36; *37*
France, *13*
Francis of Assisi, *12*
Franklin, Benjamin, 17
French knot, 65; *65, 67*

G

geometric motifs, 134
Germany:
    calligraphy, *13*
    samplers, 109
    tablecloths, *17*
gingham borders, 80; *80-1*
gingham tablecloths, 97; *96-7*
Glubb, Charlotte, *110*
Gower, Anne, *111*
Greece:
    cross stitch in, 18; *13*
    origins of cross stitch, 9
Greek stitch, 53; *51, 53*

H

Hardanger fabric, 22
Hawkins, Elisabeth, *109*
heraldic symbols, 142; *142-3*
herringbone stitch, 53; *50, 53*
    closed, 53; *51, 53*
    double, 56; *51, 56*
    interlaced, 56; *51, 57*
    overlapping, 57; *54, 56*
    threaded, 56; *54, 56*
    tied, 56, *54; 56*
Hindu religion, *15*
Holbein stitch, 65; *65, 67*
hoops, 25; *25*
house samplers, 127-9; *12, 126-9*

I

India:
    cholas, 11, 14
    origins of cross stitch, 9
    peasant embroidery, 18; *11, 14, 38*
Indus Valley, 8
initials, samplers, 112
interlaced herringbone stitch, 56; *51, 57*
Italian stitch, 56; *54, 56-7*
Italy, *12, 137*

J

Johnston Coe, Eva, *111*
jumper, 84; *84*

K

kettle holders, *17*
key tags, 78-9
    monogram, 79
    nine-stitch, 79
knitted fabrics, 22
knotted stitch, 57, 65; *55, 57, 65*

L

lampshades, borders, 90; *90*
landscapes:
    pictures, 86; *39, 86*
    pillow covers, 72; *72*
Landseer, Sir Edwin, 17
leaf stitch, 57; *54, 57*
Lee, Alice, 106
letterforms:
    alphabet, 108, 113, 114-17; *12, 108, 114-17*
    calligraphy, *13*
    examples, *144-9*
    monograms, 138; *138-41*
Leviathan stitch, 57; *55, 57*
    double, 60; *58, 60*
lighting, 23
linen, 8, 22
linsey-woolsey, 11
long and short stitch, 65; *65, 67*
long armed cross stitch, 48; *9, 46, 47, 48*
long legged cross stitch, 48; *48*

M

Mackett, Elizabeth, *9*
Maltese Cross interlacing stitch, 60; *60*
Maltese Cross stitch, 60; *58, 60*
map samplers, 112; *109, 113*
Markham, Elizabeth, 123
Markham, Thomas, 123
materials:
    fabrics, 22
    threads, 23
matte embroidery cotton, 23
Meo tribe, *15*
Mesopotamia, 8
Mexico:
    peasant embroidery, *12*
    samplers, 110; *111*
Middle East, 10; *15*
mirrors, corner designs, 137
mitering corners, *89*
    canvas, *91*
monograms, 138; *138-41*
    designing, *139*
    examples, *153*
Montenegrin stitch, 61; *58, 59, 61*
Moshier family, *10*
Moslem religion, *15*
Mossoul stitch, 53; *53*
motifs, 133-53
    alphabets, *144-53*
    borders, 134-5; *134-7, 150-2*
    Chinese, *15*
    corners, 134-5; *134-7, 151*
    Dutch, *12*
    French, *13*
    Greek, *13, 16*
    heraldic symbols, 142; *142-3*

Indian, *14*
Italian, *12*
Mexican, *12*
monograms, 138; *138-41*
peasant, 18; *15, 18*
Russian, *15*
samplers, 112-13
Thai, *11, 14*
Turkish, *14*
Yugoslavian, *12, 15*
motto samplers, 118-21; *118-21*
mounting, 33-6; *33-6*
Mundle, Elizabeth Rajmohani, *122*

N
napkins, 89; *88*
needles, 23
  bone, 8
  threading, 24; *24*
net appliqué, 94; *94*
Netherlands, samplers, 109-10; *12*
Nile Valley, 8
Noyes, Lydia, Martha, *9*

O
oblong cross stitch, 48; *46, 48-9*
oblong cross stitch with back stitch, 49; *46, 49*
origins of embroidery, 8-9
overalls, pocket and patches, 85; *85*
overlapping herringbone stitch, 56; *54, 56*

P
Palestinians, *15*
pattern books, 107-8
pearl cotton, 23
peasant embroidery, 18; *15, 18*
Persia, 9
Persian wool, 23
Pether, Mary, 127; *127*
petit point, 65; *65*
photograph frames, 93; *93*
pictures, 11
  landscape, 86; *39, 86*
pillowcases, borders, 92; *92*
pillow covers, 72-5; *12, 72-5*

checkerboard motif, 74-5
cording, 73
landscape design, 72; *72*
striped panels, 74
pincushions, 82-3; *62, 82-3*
  block pattern, 83; *83*
  crazywork, 82; *82*
plaited Slav stitch, 48; *48*
plant motifs, *12, 13*
  samplers, 112
plumage stitch, 65; *65*
plush stitch, 64; *16, 64*
pockets, 85, *85*
portraiture, 17
pressing, 31-2; *31*
projects, 70-103
  samplers, 114-31
purse, repeat patterns, 87; *87*

R
religious texts, 118-19
religious vestments, 9; *10*
repeat pattern purse, 87; *87*
rice stitch, 61; *58, 61*
Rich, Barnabe, 106
Richards, Mary Anne, *107*
Richardson, Eliza, *119*
Roberson, Charlotte, 118
rococo stitch, 11, 61; *9, 58, 61, 62*
Romanian stitch, 65; *65*
Rome, 8, 9
rotating frames, 26; *26*
Royal School of Needlework, 17
Russia, 9, 15
Russian cross stitch, 53; *53*
Russian stitch, 53; *53*

S
St Francis of Assisi, *12*
St George cross stitch, 49; *46, 49*
sampler stitch, 44, 107; *44*
samplers, 65-131
  alphabet, 108, 113, 114-17; *12, 108, 114-17*
  American, 111, 112, 127, 128, 130; *12, 110-11*
  band, *9, 106, 107*
  changing form of, 108-9
  design, 107-8, 112-13
  designing, 112-13
  English, 106-9; *59, 106-9*
  European, 109-10
  family tree, 123-5; *122-5*
  house, 127-9; *12, 126-9*
  map, 112; *109, 113*

motto, 118-21; *118-21*
projects, 114-31
sewing, *112*
stitch, 130-1; *130-1*
satin stitch, 8, 10, 65; *9, 65, 67*
scale, borders, 135
scroll frames, 26; *26*
sequins, *11*
sewing samplers, *112*
shading stitch, 65; *65*
shadow stitch, 53; *53*
shawls, *12*
sheets, borders, 92; *92*
shirts, 77
Shoreleyker, 108
skirts:
  decorative gingham border, 80; *80-1*
  Thai, *14*
slippers, *8*
Society for Decorative Arts, 17
Soviet Union, 9; *15*
Spain, 9
  samplers, 110
spinning, early, 8
Standish, Loara, 111
Stanwood Bolton, Ethel, 111
stitch sampler, 130-1; *130-1*
stitches, 41-67
  alternate cross stitch, 45; *42, 45*
  backstitch, 64; *63, 64*
  basket stitch, 44; *42, 44*
  closed herringbone stitch, 53; *51, 53*
  cross stitch, 44, 107; *42, 44, 45*
  crossed corners cross stitch, 61; *61*
  diagonal cross stitch, 45; *42, 45*
  dot stitch, 65; *65*
  double back stitch, 53; *53*
  double cross stitch, 45; *45, 46*
  double herringbone stitch, 56; *51, 56*
  double Leviathan stitch, 60; *58, 60*
  double running stitch, 65; *9, 65*
  double sided cross stitch, 48; *46, 48*
  ermine stitch, 52; *50, 52*
  fern stitch, 52; *50, 52*
  fishbone stitch, 52; *50, 52*
  flat stitch, 52; *50, 52-3*
  for canvas, 67
  for common-weave fabrics, 67
  for even-weave fabrics, 67
  French knot, 65; *65, . 67*
  Greek stitch, 53; *51, 53*
  herringbone stitch, 53; *50, 53*
  Holbein stitch, 65; *65, 67*
  interlaced herringbone stitch, 56; *51, 57*
  Italian stitch, 56; *54, 56-7*
  knotted stitch, 57, 65; *55, 57, 65*
  leaf stitch, 57; *54, 57*
  Leviathan stitch, 57; *55, 57*

long and short stitch, 65; *65,
67*
long armed cross stitch, 48; *9,
46, 47, 48*
long legged cross stitch, 48; *48*
Maltese Cross interlacing
stitch, 60; *60*
Maltese Cross stitch, 60; *58,
60*
Montenegrin stitch, 61; *58, 59,
61*
Mossoul stitch, 53; *53*
oblong cross stitch, 48; *46,
48-9*
oblong cross stitch with back
stitch, 49; *46, 49*
overlapping herringbone
stitch, 56; *54, 56*
petit point, 65; *65*
plaited Slav stitch, 48; *48*
plumage stitch, 65; *65*
plush stitch, 64; *16, 64*
rice stitch, 61; *58, 61*
Russian cross stitch, 53; *53*
Russian stitch, 53; *53*
St George cross stitch, 49; *46,
49*
sampler stitch, 44, 107; *44*
satin stitch, 8, 10, 65; *9, 65,
67*
shading stitch, 65; *65*
shadow stitch, 53; *53*
stroke stitch, 65; *65*
tent stitch, 10, 65; *65, 67*
threaded herringbone stitch,
56; *54, 56*
tied herringbone stitch, 56; *54,
56*
Torocko stitch, 64; *63, 64*
two-sided Italian cross stitch,
9
underlined stitch, 64; *63, 64*
velvet stitch, 64; *16, 63, 64, 66*
William and Mary stitch, 61;
61
stranded floss, 23
stranded pure silk, 23
stretchers, 26; *26*
mounting, 33; *33*
stroke stitch, 65; *65*
Sumerians, 8
Syon Cope, 9

T

tablecloths, 89; *88-9*
German, *17*
gingham, 97; *96-7*
tapestry needles, 23
tapestry yarn, 23
tent stitch, 10, 65; *65, 67*
textiles, *see* fabrics
texture:
and color, *39*

borders, 135
samplers, 113
Thailand:
contemporary embroidery, *11*
peasant embroidery, *14, 15*
threaded herringbone stitch, 56;
54, 56
threads, 23
colors, 38
early, 8
finishing, 24
for heraldic devices, 142
preparing, 24; *24*
starting, 24
tied herringbone stitch, 56; *54, 56*
Tiffany, Louis, 17
Tipper, M.A., *108*
Torocko stitch, 64; *63, 64*
tracing designs, 27; *27*
transferring designs, 27-9, 108; *27,
28*
Turkey, *14*
Turkey work, *16*
two-sided Italian cross stitch, *9*

U

underlined stitch, 64; *63, 64*
United States of America,
cross stitch, 10, 11, 17; *16*
*samplers, 111, 112, 127, 128,
130; 12, 110-11*

V

valances, 12, *13,*
Van Reed Gresemer, Rebecca, *110*
velvet stitch, 64; *16, 63, 64, 66*
vestments, church, 9; *10*
Vincentio, 108

W

wall hangings, *10*
Washington, George, 17
weaving: early, 8
see also fabrics
West Germany, *13*
Wheeler, Candace, 17
whitework samplers, 108; *107*
William and Mary stitch, 61; *61*
wool, early use, 8

Y

Yao tribe, *15*
yarns, 23
Yugoslavia, *12, 15, 18*

Acknowledgments

The pictures on these pages were reproduced by courtesy of the following:

8, 9 *(b)* Victoria and Albert Museum; **9** *(t)*, **(10)** *(br)* Martin Gostelow/Daughters of the American Revolution Museum, Washington; **(10)** *(tl, bl, tr)* Victoria and Albert Museum; **11** *(l)* Chris Rushton, *(r)* John Gillow; **12** The American Museum, Bath; **13** *(t, c, b, bl)* Victoria and Albert Museum, *(bl)* Eirian Short; **14** *(r)* Jan Eaton; **14** *(c, b)*, **15** *(t)* Goldsmith's College Textile Collection; **15** *(b)* Marion Appleton; **16** *(b)* The Bridgman Art Library/Smithsonian Institute, Washington; **17** *(r)* Victoria and Albert Museum; **17** *(l)*, **18** Goldsmith's College Textile Collection; **19** John Gillow; **38** Goldsmith's College Textile Collection; **39** Liz Mundle; **43, 46, 59, 62, 66, 101** Victoria and Albert Museum; **106, 107** *(l)* Fitzwilliam Museum, Cambridge; **107** *(r)*, **108** *(t)* Victoria and Albert Museum; **108** *(b)*, **109** *(r)* Fitzwilliam Museum, Cambridge; **109** *(l)* **110** *(b)* Victoria and Albert Museum; **110** *(t)*, **111** The American Museum, Bath; **112, 113** Fitzwilliam Museum, Cambridge; **114** The Danish House; **119** Victoria and Albert Museum; **123** The Danish House; **127, 137** Victoria and Albert Museum; **144-153** Quill Publishing Limited/Dover Publications, Inc, New York.

All other photographs property of Quill Publishing Limited.

Key: *(t)* top; *(b)* below; *(l)* left; *(r)* right; *(c)* center.

While every effort has been made to acknowledge all copyright holders, we apologize if any omissions have been made.